The Evolution of American Foreign Policy

CONTENTS

The Evolution of American Foreign Policy

scan the figures of patents applied for in the *Statistical Abstract of the United States* and compare these figures with those of any other country, to see that there exists among the American people a peculiar aptitude for living in a technological age and operating a high-powered technological society. The conditions in this respect may change; the growth of new philosophies may in time seriously affect the efficiency of the American order; the forces of social unrest may become more serious than they have been in the past; but, viewing the matter in historical perspective, it is clear that while much is due, in the building of the American nation, to the gifts of nature (and more than Americans are commonly willing to assume), much is also due to an active, energetic, and inventive people. One of the sources of American national strength is the readiness with which the people of the United States (conservative in their political cast of thought) welcome technical and scientific changes, are eager to increase the efficiency of their industrial processes, and are zealous to take advantage of the widening frontiers of scientific knowledge.

Finally, one of the sources of American strength has been the growth of a vigorous managerial class that has manned the American industrial machine with remarkable competence. The development of such a class has been one of the characteristics of national growth. Nowhere else in the world, it may without hazard be said, have the same opportunities been open to business enterprise that have been open in the United States. There has been much that is vulgar and selfish about the American scramble for wealth. It is by no means true that the American business class, so far as any generalization about it is possible, is always broad in its vision, hospitable to the inevitable social changes that occur in any society, understanding of the problems of international life. But in its own sphere it is worthy of great praise. The conduct of a great industrial machine calls for the highest managerial qualities. These qualities have not been wanting in the United States. Indeed, any careful student who compares American business genius with that of Britain or of France, to take two obvious examples, cannot fail to suspect, I will not say perceive, that entrepreneurial and managerial enterprise is more highly developed in the first case than in the other two. And in the modern world, in which war has become so largely a matter of technology, this is of transcendent importance. No student of America's place in the international world can afford to neglect these important considerations.

Let us now sum up the generalizations with which we have been concerned. A large population, but a population not too large for the area that it inhabits, immense natural resources, a peculiar aptitude in the field of practical invention, and a not inconsiderable ability to develop a managerial class that, in its limited field, is effective and vigorous, these have been the sources of American strength and the secret of American rise into the position of a world power. These are the bare bones of the story, however. The process of expansion, the widening area of American diplomatic action, the influence of the United States in the world today are only to be discovered by a survey of the history of its foreign policy. It is to such a survey that this book is dedicated.

II   TERRITORIAL EXPANSION

FUNDAMENTAL to an understanding of the development of American foreign policy is a knowledge of the process by which the United States attained its present extent on the American continent. Almost every stage of this process raised a diplomatic problem; and some of these problems were of peculiar interest in the development of the nation. There is, indeed, no story quite like the story of American expansion; and to tell that story in its broad lines is the object of the present chapter.

We have said that at the time of the American Revolution the population of the thirteen colonies was for the most part confined to the eastern slope of the Alleghenies; yet the United States began its history as a nation with a much wider area. How did it happen that, at the conclusion of the war with Britain, it was possible to define the boundaries of the United States in much more generous terms, to limit its domain on the West by the line of the Mississippi, and thus early in the national existence to enable it to obtain control of a substantial territory?

The existence of a territorial appetite on the part of the people of the United States is coincident with, or indeed anterior to, their birth as a nation. In the year 1775, before the Declaration of Independence was issued, the Americans, in the course of their hostilities against Great Britain, attempted an invasion of Canada. The effort failed; the famous battle of the snows before the citadel of Quebec, fought at the very end of 1775, dashed American hopes, and never again during the war were American troops to appear on Canadian soil. The loyalty of the French priests to Great Britain, the tactless behavior of the Americans, the proffer of a debauched currency in exchange for supplies, all tended to defeat an enterprise that the fortunes of war decidedly vetoed; but the ambition that the whole

9

project displayed is interesting evidence of the expansionist views of Americans. Nor is it without interest that, on the signing of the French alliance of 6 February 1778, Canada was definitely excluded from the sphere of French activities and reserved for the conquest of the United States. Finally, the colossal assurance of Benjamin Franklin permitted him, in the course of the peace negotiations, to suggest the cession of this British province, in which there was not a single American soldier, on the grounds that such action would tend to produce a reconciliation between the mother country and its rebellious colonies. In the light of facts like these, it is not surprising that, in the course of discussions that terminated the Revolutionary War, the Americans should naturally look to the enlargement of their national domain to whatever extent the fortunes of war and the skill of their diplomats might make feasible.

But in the negotiations of peace, there was certainly nothing inevitable about the excellent results that Franklin and Adams and Jay, the negotiators of the peace, actually secured. The trans-Appalachian West, from the mountains to the Mississippi, was not, for the most part, in American hands. It is true that George Rogers Clark, in an expedition that was one of the most celebrated and one of the most daring in the history of the Revolution, had penetrated into the old Northwest and had surprised the garrisons maintained by the British at the posts of Kaskaskia, Cahokia, and Vincennes. But before the end of the war Clark had withdrawn to the falls of the Ohio, while a British garrison occupied the important post of Detroit. Looked at from the point of view of physical possession, therefore, the British would have been able, if they had desired, to make out an excellent claim to the Western country, and it is not easy to see how such a claim, if put forward, could have been successfully resisted. The colonies were weak; they were still distraught; they would have found it hard to rouse their inhabitants to battle for the West.

There was also another contestant in the field. Spain had entered the Revolutionary War against Britain in 1779. She had, before the end of the struggle, easily overrun Florida, which had been held by the British since 1763. She had her eyes on the territory that extended from the borders of Florida to the Ohio. She had made this fact clear to France, her associate in the conflict just ending and her close diplomatic ally, and she had certainly not been discouraged by the French foreign minister, Vergennes. She was already engaged in intrigue with the Indians of this territory and seeking to bring it under her influence. She was, indeed (and very logically from her own point of view), anxious to limit American power and to secure for herself an additional area that would protect her vast holdings in the Southwest, especially the province of Louisiana and the port of New Orleans. She had been at no time very sympathetic with the American Revolutionary cause, nor was there any reason for her, the possessor of a vast colonial domain, to look with complacency upon the growth of a new revolutionary power in the New World.

Why was it then, we repeat, that the United States was able, in the treaty of peace, to secure a vast region stretching from the Great Lakes to the line of 31°, and to begin its career as a nation with this great and important expanse of territory already in its hands. The answer lies primarily in the complacency of the British Ministry. It is true that the American negotiators at Paris, Franklin and Adams and Jay, were men of great ability. It is true that they showed a striking independence of mind, and that they very wisely deviated from that part of their instructions which would have made them unduly dependent on the advice of the French foreign minister. But these facts would not have been controlling, in all probability, had it not been for the attitude of the British Cabinet in London. The collapse of the British arms in America had resulted in the fall of the Lord North government with its rigidly conservative point of view and its dependence on the obstinate King George, and had installed in power statesmen who were by no means unsympathetic to the Americans. Great Britain, in the years of the Revolution, had found herself faced by a coalition of France, Spain, and the Netherlands, and was isolated in Europe at its close. It was the policy of Lord Shelburne, the head of the cabinet that negotiated the peace, to wean the United States away from French influence, to avoid a future conflict over Western expansion, and to give to his own country, weakened by a long war, an opportunity once more to consolidate its power. There were many Englishmen who did not agree with him. Indeed, under the storm of criticism awakened by the American treaty his ministry fell; but the work that it had done remained; and it is a fact of substantial interest that, this early in the history of Anglo-American relations, a conciliatory spirit toward the United States expressed itself in the foreign policy of Britain. This was not always to be so; but, on the other hand, the attitude of the Shelburne ministry has, as we shall see, more than one counterpart in the future relations of the two countries.

Thus the United States began its history as a considerable state, with a substantial national domain. Yet it was surrounded by European neighbors. On the north was the British province of Canada, divided from the young republic for the most part by the line of the Lakes; on the West was the vast province of Louisiana, in the hands of Spain; and on the south was Florida, which had been rewon by the Spaniards from Britain in the war just ended. In which direction would the expansive energies of the American Republic first turn? How and when would the American domain be next enlarged?

The answer was to lie in the acquisition of Louisiana. But in order to understand this remarkable episode, it is necessary to begin with some background material. In the years following the establishment of the National government, the pioneers were busily overflowing the trans-Appalachian region. Within seven years two new states had been admitted to the union, Kentucky in 1792 and Tennessee in 1796. The inhabitants of these regions were accustomed, in days when no road system existed, to float their produce down the Ohio and the Mississippi to the port of New Orleans, where it was transshipped to ocean-going vessels. For the carrying on of this lucrative commerce, the 'right of deposit' at New Orleans was vital, and, for the ensuring of this right, it was necessary to make an arrangement with Spain. For some time after 1789 the Spaniards can hardly be said to have behaved with much cordiality toward the United States. They intrigued constantly with the Southern Indians, and declined all overtures from the American government. But, as was frequently to happen in the early years of the Republic, the outbreak of the wars of the French Revolution in Europe redounded to the interest of the Americans. Spain had originally entered this conflict on the side of Britain against revolutionary France. But increasingly jealous of the mistress of the seas, the Spanish ministry, dominated by the royal favorite Godoy, first made peace with France and then shifted to the French side. To protect itself in such circumstances against Great Britain, to prevent a possible coalition of Britain and America (a contingency not beyond Spanish imagination in 1795), it negotiated with Thomas Pinckney the famous treaty of 1795, which conceded the right of deposit, provided for the Spanish recognition of the line of 31° as the northern boundary of Florida, and contained a Spanish pledge to refrain from tampering with the Indians. This agreement satisfied for the time being the economic necessities of the

Western frontiersmen, and it was its violation that produced the diplomatic crisis that led to the cession of Louisiana.

The story is one of the most interesting and dramatic in the annals of the United States. Louisiana, at the end of the eighteenth century, belonged to Spain. But Napoleon Bonaparte, who came to power in France in 1799, began his career as the ruler of the French with a policy of peace and colonial expansion. By a treaty that was made in October of 1800, the Spaniards were induced to cede to France a province they found costly and burdensome, in exchange for the promise of an Italian kingdom for one of the scions of the house of Bourbon. Such a transaction, which involved the transfer of an important area from the hands of a weak to the hands of a strong power, could not fail to interest the United States. It was some time before the treaty became known. Yet, as early as the spring of 1802, Thomas Jefferson, no Francophobe and certainly no militarist, wrote a famous letter in which he declared that the day that France took possession of New Orleans the Americans must marry themselves to the British fleet and the British nation. No statesman, however pacific, could have watched with indifference a transaction of such great moment.

The crisis came, however, only with the suspension by Spain, in direct violation of the treaty of 1795 and while she was still in posession of Louisiana, of the right of deposit. Instantly the Western country was aflame; the Federalists, out of power and eager, as the 'outs' have often been in American history, to capitalize a question of foreign policy, began to talk of war; and a very serious situation was obviously developing. But Jefferson, whose *sang-froid* was equal to almost any occasion, instead of indulging in rodomontade, sent a special envoy to France in the person of his friend and protégé, James Monroe. Monroe had endeared himself to the West by his strong support of the freedom of the navigation of the Mississippi in the days of the Confederation; the danger of an explosion in trans-Appalachia was allayed by his appointment, and a relative calm descended upon the country while the result of his mission was awaited.

The mission came out far differently from what any one could have expected, and far differently from what the administration in Washington intended. Jefferson and Madison, his Secretary of State, had little interest in Louisiana; what they wanted was New Orleans, with a slice of territory to the eastward (what was then called West

Florida); and they were ready (most unwisely, as it looks in the perspective of today) to guarantee the trans-Mississippi region to France if they could make a good bargain on these other points. Napoleon, it developed, had other views and intentions. His colonial adventure had turned out badly; he had poured out money and men in the conquest of the former French colony of Santo Domingo without success; and by the spring of 1803 his relations with England were worsening, and the prospects of war were increasing. In a sudden and dramatic alteration of policy, he authorized his foreign minister, Talleyrand, to offer all of Louisiana to the United States, including the island of New Orleans. This offer was made to Livingston, the American minister at Paris, the day before Monroe reached the French capital. The two Americans were, it must be admitted, not wholly without jealousy of each other in the negotiations that followed; but both were wise enough to ignore or to transcend their instructions and, after a period of diplomatic haggling, they signed a treaty for the cession of Louisiana.

This famous compact is interesting from a variety of points of view. It was negotiated by Napoleon without his ever having fulfilled the condition of the transfer of the province from Spain to France (that is, the creation of an Italian kingdom for one of the Bourbons). It was also signed in violation of an explicit assurance given by Bonaparte to the Spanish Court that Louisiana would never be alienated to any other power. It was signed in defiance of the French Constitution and of a substantial body of French public opinion. It was framed in terms so ambiguous, with regard to the definition of boundaries, as to lead to much trouble in the future, and as to permit the American negotiators to assume that they had bought West Florida, or a substantial part of it, as well as the trans-Mississippi region. But Livingston and Monroe were not inclined to look a gift horse in the mouth; and none of these things, in so far as they were known to them, acted as a deterrent to their conclusion of the treaty. They had, indeed, transacted the greatest real estate deal in history; they had bought an area larger than the original area of the United States for a price that works out at about three cents an acre. If ever in diplomatic history there was a case of good fortune unprecedented in its extent, it was that which befell the two American negotiators. And once again, as in the peace negotiations of 1781-83, the United States had profited from the divisions and the rivalries of Europe.

It is interesting to observe the fortunes of the treaty on its arrival in Washington. Jefferson, at first, was somewhat taken aback at the action of his envoys. He had not contracted to buy half a continent, and he was disposed to believe that a constitutional amendment was necessary to make the transaction legal. But Jefferson, despite his theories, was rarely a doctrinaire when practical values were at stake; and in due course he decided to overlook 'metaphysical subtleties' and urge ratification. Less admirable was the attitude of the Federalists. In the fall of 1802 and the winter of 1803, they had talked as if they were ready to go to war for New Orleans; now they opposed the treaty that made war unnecessary. They were the party of broad construction; now they talked in terms of a violation of the Constitution. Their antics did no real harm; but they illustrate a fact that is of more than passing interest and of melancholy import in the field of American foreign policy; that is, that until very recently partisanship has again and again been present in a virulent form in matters that concern the nation's external affairs. So secure was the position of the United States in the nineteenth century that this expensive luxury could be indulged in, it must be admitted; but the precedents of an earlier time are certainly not a desirable guide for the diplomacy of the age in which we live.

There is one concluding point concerning the purchase of Louisiana that must not be allowed to escape the attention of the reader. The purchase price was large for those times, $15,000,000, and much of it had to be borrowed. It was found in London, and found there after war had actually begun between France and Britain; the powerful house of Baring Brothers was actually permitted by the British Government to lend to the United States $10,000,000 which were in due course to be turned over to the relentless Bonaparte. This act of complacency deserves more attention than it has received from the diplomatic historians.

The acquisition of Louisiana furnishes the prelude to the Florida question. On *West* Florida Jefferson had his eye from the beginning. By a strained construction of the Treaty of Paris, it was possible to claim that the United States, by cession from France, had acquired the region eastward of the Great River as far as the Perdido. Over it the United States asserted jurisdiction as early as 1804, to the great rage of the Spaniards; and only a little later Jefferson attempted to secure its cession from Spain by persuading France to bully the Court of Madrid into acquiescence, in the hope of France itself profiting pecuniarily from the transaction. But this rather shoddy maneuver got nowhere, and it was left to Madison to acquire a part of West Florida by methods that were, perhaps, hardly less reprehensible than those of his mentor and predecessor in the Presidency. American settlers had, by 1810, moved over the line into Spanish territory. There a separatist movement soon appeared that was encouraged, if not actively assisted, by the administration in Washington. A short-lived revolution brought into being the republic of West Florida, which speedily applied for annexation to the United States. On 10 October 1810, Madison issued a proclamation extending American jurisdiction over the territory, and most of it was occupied. It was only in 1813, however, when the Spanish situation was even more distressful than in 1810, that the city of Mobile was taken possession of. In its handling of this matter, the American regime certainly showed no sign of sympathy with a weak power that was fighting for its national independence against the towering ambition of the Corsican.

But the rest of Florida to the east of the Perdido was to remain for a time in the hands of Spain. It was of substantial importance to the United States, since the backwoodsmen of Georgia and Alabama used the river systems of the Southeast to ship their produce to the sea, just as those of Kentucky and Tennessee used the Mississippi. Moreover, it may be said in all justice that the weakness of Spain gave to the Indians of Florida a peculiar capacity to annoy the American settlers, while in the War of 1812 British adventurers did not fail to play a part in troubling the border, and an official British force appeared at Pensacola. In circumstances such as these, it is not strange that the acquisition of the province became the objective of Madison and of Monroe. In 1812 the administration attempted to repeat the *coup* that had brought it the western part of the province; and one George Mathews, an illiterate former Governor of Georgia, was encouraged to co-operate with American insurgents to the south of the border. But the offensive against the Spanish post of St. Augustine bogged down; the revolution was so feeble that it had to be disavowed by the embarrassed conspirators in Washington; and in due course the American troops who had crossed the frontier were withdrawn.

It was left, then, to John Quincy Adams, Secretary of State in the Monroe administration, to complete the Florida enterprise by methods more straightforward than those employed by his predecessor.

Picking up negotiations already begun when he entered office during 1817 and 1818, Adams was engaged in prolix arguments intended to persuade declining Spain to give up a province that she held only with difficulty. For a time the progress made was slight; but a famous incident precipitated, as it would appear, a favorable decision. In 1817, Andrew Jackson, the hero of New Orleans, was sent to the Florida border with instructions to protect the settlers against the Indians and even to pursue the troublesome red men into Spanish territory if they sought refuge there. Jackson believed that his authority was still wider; he seems to have thought that he had been authorized to seize the province, and, with his strong prejudice against both Spaniards and Indians, it was not difficult for him to act upon this assumption. In the spring of 1818, he burst into Florida, occupied St. Marks and Pensacola, confiscated the royal archives, deposed the Spanish governor, executed two British subjects accused of complicity with the Indians, and declared in force 'the revenue laws of the United States,' all in a breathless few weeks. There were many who condemned the impulsive General's action, and most of Monroe's cabinet were not disposed to defend it; but, however reprehensible it may have seemed—or been—it was probably the very thing needed to convince the Spaniards that they had better make a virtue of necessity and cede a province that, it was obvious, they could hardly hope to retain. At any rate, the negotiations that had notably lagged acquired a new velocity in the months that followed, and had their issue in a treaty signed on 22 February 1819.

In the discussions of this treaty, however, Spain was not without diplomatic cards, and these were played with considerable skill by Onís, the experienced Spanish minister in Washington. In exchange for her consent to the cession, the Spaniard demanded a settlement of the western boundary of Louisiana on terms favorable to the Court of Madrid. This boundary, like that on the east, was subject to conflicting interpretations of the treaty of 1803; it was possible, by the construction most favorable to the Americans, to fix the line on the Rio Grande, but, by the least favorable construction, on the Sabine, which forms the eastern boundary of Texas today. How it should run from the Gulf of Mexico northward was a question that gave ample room for difference of opinion, and on these points Onís and Adams wrangled in the fall and winter of 1818-19. On the whole, the result was a compromise. Adams gave up Texas; the frontier ran by a zigzag line to the Rockies; and then it passed along the 42nd parallel to the Pacific. By this latter delimitation Spain gave up her claims to the territory broadly known as Oregon; and the American Secretary of State, surveying with pride the results of his labors and seeking perhaps to console himself for the surrender of the Southwest, declared that his 'continental treaty' marked an 'epocha' in the history of his country. He had a right to be proud of it; though later to be denounced as an unjustifiable surrender of American rights, it was at the time almost universally praised, and it was ratified by the Senate by a unanimous vote, an event that at any time and in any age deserves commemoration.

There were difficulties before the proud and obstinate government of Spain accepted the results of its own negotiator; an annoying delay occurred before the treaty was ratified; but Adams's tenacity triumphed over all difficulties; and the treaty, whose time limit had expired, was again submitted to the Senate and again ratified on 19 February 1821, with only four dissenting votes. Thus another important area was added to the territory of the United States.

By the treaty of 1821, the United States had renounced its claims to Texas. It was not so very long, however, before the Texan question was to be revived and was to play an important part in both the foreign and domestic politics of the Americans. And in some respects the question of Texas is like the question of West Florida. In both cases, American settlers oozed over a frontier line into territory that was not American; in both cases they became restive under another jurisdiction; in both cases revolution broke out and a proclamation of independence followed. But here the similarity ends. For in the case of Texas, the American administration in power indulged in no such intrigues as those connected with the matter of the Floridas; nor did it hasten to take possession of the region, once the revolutionary movement was completed. But let us look at the initial facts in this problem a little more closely.

By the revolution that took place in 1822, Mexico succeeded Spain, now decrepit, in the sovereignty of Texas. Following the example of the former mother-country, the Mexican government at first encouraged American settlement and thus prepared the way for its own undoing. Repenting too late of its action, it sought in vain to control the settlers; and the revolt that followed could have but one result. On the field of San Jacinto, the picturesque Sam Houston and his followers won the independence of his country. There can be little question that the Texan revolution received unofficial support from American sources, and that along the border public sentiment was warmly in favor of the revolutionists. But it seems equally certain that the attitude of the Jackson administration was, on the whole, that of a correct neutrality, and it is undebatable that Old Hickory and his cabinet moved in the Texan question with great caution. The reasons for this circumspection are not far to seek. Texas was slave territory, and with the middle eighteen-thirties the slavery question was beginning to loom large in American politics. In addition a presidential election was at hand (the year was 1836), and the occupant of the White House was anxious to transmit the presidency to his friend, Martin Van Buren. The recognition of Texas was therefore postponed until March 1837, on the eve of Van Buren's assumption of the office of Chief Executive.

The 'little magician,' as the new President was called, was a cautious, albeit an honest and competent, political leader. Accordingly, the overtures of Texas for admission to the Union were discouraged, and the question slumbered throughout his whole presidential term. Nor did matters change at once when the Whigs came into power in 1841. The Secretary of State in the new administration was Daniel Webster of Massachusetts, and as long as he remained in charge of American foreign policy it was safe to say that the problem of Texan annexation would be avoided.

By 1843, however, the situation was altered. Webster resigned and President Tyler, a Virginian and a friend of annexation, appointed as Webster's successor in the State Department Abel P. Upshur. To these two men an independent Texas meant a Texas in close relations with Great Britain—a Texas that might be used by that nefarious power (for so they both were inclined to regard it) against the United States. And there was, indeed, some ground for their dislike of close relations between the Lone Star Republic and the British. British abolitionists hoped to persuade the Texans to abolish slavery; and beyond all doubt many other Britons, and some of them in the Foreign Office, saw an opportunity to acquire a market for their manufactures, to provide themselves with a source of raw cotton, to free themselves from their dangerous dependence on the United States, and, by adopting free trade policies, to encourage the tariff-burdened Southern states to make a breach in the protectionist wall that had been erected in the United States. Faced by what he regarded as a British peril, Secretary Upshur began negotiations for annexation, and when he was killed by the explosion of a gun on the warship *Princeton* in February 1844, his successor, John C. Calhoun, the most determined advocate of Southern interests, took up the thread of the diplomatic conversations. So anxious for a positive result was the new Secretary, that he sought to assure the Texans that they would be protected against a possible attack from Mexico (which had not recognized Texan independence and was still at war with the Republic) by the stationing of American vessels in the Gulf and the dispatch of American troops to the border. But Calhoun, despite his high abilities, seriously bungled the whole problem. He was taking great risks in bringing up a treaty of annexation in a presidential year in any case; but he immensely increased his difficulties by the famous dispatch to Pakenham, the British minister, which saw the light in the spring of 1844. In this dispatch, which was addressed as much to home as to foreign opinion, Calhoun, in discussing the Texan matter, defended American slavery in the warmest terms and thus made more unlikely than ever the ratification of the compact. The Senate voted in June; the Northern vote was almost solidly against favorable action; the Southern Whigs joined their Northern colleagues (for by this time Tyler was, if anything, a Democrat, and no longer commanded the loyalty of his former party associates), and annexation was defeated by the crushing vote of 35 to 16.

The Texan issue was bound to figure largely in the campaign that followed. The Democratic party, both through its platform and through the voice of its candidate, endorsed Texan annexation in the clearest language. Henry Clay, the candidate of the Whigs, resorted to political equivocations that alienated some of the antislavery men of the North and probably lost him the election. And now a remarkable thing occurred. *Demos* had spoken. The same Congress that had rejected annexation in June was to accept it in its concluding session. In the Senate, it is true, there were not enough votes for the ratification of a treaty. But the friends of Texas resorted to an expedient that demonstrated, for the first time, how a minority of the Upper House of Congress might be outflanked. Texas was admitted to the Union as a state by a joint resolution of *both* Houses. The bill was signed by President Tyler on 1 March 1845, and in July Texas itself accepted the terms of the measure and added itself to the American galaxy.

The final consummation of this result was not accomplished,

nevertheless, without some pretty active opposition on the part of Britain and France. In 1844 Lord Aberdeen, the British Foreign Secretary, seemed to be ready, in concert with the Court of the Tuileries, to guarantee the independence of Texas against the United States, and even to fight to maintain it. Reports from Washington cooled his ardor as time went on, but in the winter of 1845 an earnest effort was made to persuade Mexico to recognize Texan independence, on the assurance that Texas would remain independent. This in part succeeded; an offer along these lines was made. Confronted, however, with a choice between independence and Mexican recognition on the one hand, and incorporation in the Union on the other, the Texans had little hesitation in opting for the latter.

The acquisition of the Lone Star State was, at the time, and has been since, the subject of much criticism. But such criticism seems hardly just. Texan independence was a fact, after 1836. The United States waited virtually for nine years before annexation. There was no doubt about the sentiment of the Texans themselves. American interest demanded that a strong independent state should not develop in the South that might exercise a pull on the Southern members of the Union. It may be safely affirmed that no great nation would have acted otherwise than did the Americans.

That is not to say, of course, that Mexico, the former parent-state, could be expected to enjoy what had happened. The numerous and widespread demonstrations of friendship for Texas in the period of the revolution had been irritating enough. The action finally taken ignored the fact that Mexico still had claims on Texas; and it was followed by the withdrawal of the Mexican minister from Washington. Thus the Texan question led on toward the Mexican War.

This war has been frequently treated as one of unqualified aggression. It is probably true that had the United States practiced the maximum restraint, conflict might have been avoided. But the course of events with regard to it seems to show that President Polk, while by no means emollient in his attitude, was willing to come to a settlement with Mexico that might have saved that country—at least for the time being—from the losses that it then incurred. When his administration began, there was an unsettled boundary controversy between the American government and its new neighbor. There were also outstanding many claims against the Mexican government, which that government had agreed to pay, but upon which it had defaulted. First assuring himself, as he thought, that an American minister would be received in Mexico City, Polk sent John Slidell of Louisiana to the city of the Montezumas. Slidell's instructions authorized him to offer a settlement of the differences between the two nations, balancing the claims and a money payment against possible acquisition of territory. The minimum settlement outlined called for the recognition of the line of the Rio Grande boundary, in exchange for which only the claims themselves would be assumed; but Slidell might offer $5,000,000 for New Mexico, and he might offer $25,-000,000 for New Mexico and California. The Louisianan, when he arrived in Mexico City, was not received; the Mexican government claimed that he came as a full-fledged envoy and not as the mere commissioner with whom it had engaged itself to carry on conversations; and, whether we accept this ingenious explanation or not, it is certain that the violence of Mexican feeling would in any case have made negotiation difficult if not impossible. Indeed, while Slidell was at the capital, the relatively mild Herrera regime was overthrown by a militantly reactionary and nationalist group, and his attempt once more to open up conversations was a stark failure.

These facts, it seems clear, determined the hard and resolute man in Washington toward war; but, before his decision had been definitely made, a border incident offered a convenient basis for action. There was, as we have seen, a frontier controversy between Texas and Mexico, involving the strip of territory between the river Nueces and the Rio Grande. After Slidell's second failure to establish relations, Polk ordered General Taylor to occupy this region. The General did so, advancing to the second-named river, and even, in excess of zeal, establishing a naval blockade of the river, thus preventing the Mexicans from communicating by water with Matamoros on the southern bank. The Mexicans then crossed the river and a skirmish occurred. The news of these events arrived in Washington just as Polk was considering his message. He acted at once, and, declaring (quite inaccurately) that American blood had been shed upon American soil, demanded of Congress a declaration of war.

Thus began the American war that aroused the maximum amount of criticism at home. To the anti-slavery men of the North, the conflict was one of naked aggression, having as its aim the extension of slave territory. 'They jest want this Californy so's to lug new slave states in,' wrote James Russell Lowell. There seems little truth in this charge. That Polk had his eye on California is true. That he had instructed the American consul at Monterey to stimulate sentiment for annexation was also true. That he was free from acquisitive instincts no one would deny. But there is no evidence that he was acting from any friendship for slavery, and it is not to be forgotten that Slidell was instructed to accept a settlement with Mexico that would have, for the time being, left that province in the hands of the Dons. It is still possible to criticize his course as lacking in the essential patience that a strong nation should show toward a relatively weak one. But it is only fair to say that Mexican opinion was fully as bellicose as that of the United States; that Mexico had refused what might have been a reasonable opportunity to settle outstanding questions between the two nations; and that it was imprudent of the Mexican government to refuse. On the other hand, the order to Taylor to occupy disputed territory was a provocative act; and Taylor's conduct was no less so. While abstaining then from the unqualified partisan condemnation that was at the time visited upon Polk by the Whigs, it is fair to say that the circumstances surrounding the outbreak of war are not such as to satisfy in every respect the scrupulous friend of national honor and self-restraint.

Victory for the United States in the struggle that opened in April 1846 was foreshadowed. By September 1847 General Scott had entered Mexico City, and California had been overrun. The negotiations for peace were, in many respects, most interesting, indeed, almost without precedent. Accompanying General Scott as he advanced on Mexico City was a special agent of the State Department, Nicholas Trist. But the administration became dissatisfied with the results of Trist's mission and got the idea that his presence was encouraging the Mexicans to prolong the war. On 7 October 1847 he was recalled. A few days later, however, he saw a chance to push negotiations. Disregarding his advices from Washington, he went ahead and concluded an unauthorized peace by which the United States got the line of the Rio Grande, New Mexico, and California, and agreed in exchange to pay $15,000,000 to Mexico and to assume the claims up to the amount of $3,250,000. The President, on receiving the news of this action, was by no means pleased at the conduct of Trist, an 'impudent and unqualified scoundrel.' But the terms of the treaty were such as the administration had approved in April 1847; political opposition to the war was strong; a presidential election was approaching. The treaty was, therefore, submitted to the Senate; and it was ratified on 10 March 1848 by a vote of 38 to 14.

There is one other side to the Mexican War that we must consider before passing to other aspects of American expansion. That is the all-Mexico-or-none movement. An agitation along these lines developed on an increasing scale in 1847. If successful, it would have involved not the acquisition of sparsely settled territories with small alien populations, but a great adventure in the government of another people. It is fair to say that Polk in the main rejected this agitation, though he played with the idea of extending American boundaries to the south of the Rio Grande to include Chihuahua and Sonora. It is also important to note that the President's prompt submission to the Senate of Trist's treaty probably prevented the growth of what might have been a formidable propaganda for action that would have been unwise and ill-considered. His resistance to the extremists is an interesting and important historical fact.

Coincident with the Mexican War is the settlement of the Oregon controversy. This important region, from the line of 42° to 54°, had been in 1846 long claimed by both the United States and Great Britain. By the convention of 1818, it had been left open to the occupation of both. It was not until the early eighteen-forties that American settlers began to pour into the area, and that the question of a final arrangement with regard to the territory began to be raised. Great Britain was, at virtually all times, ready to settle for the 49th parallel and the Columbia. The United States wished rather to draw the boundary along the 49th parallel to the sea. The question was deadlocked at the time of the election of 1844, but the democrats inserted in their platform in that year a demand for all of Oregon, and the election cry of 'Fifty-four Forty or Fight' resounded throughout the land. But there was always an excellent chance that the question would be settled by compromise. Polk, himself no modest soul in matters of national pretension, felt obliged to offer once more the line of 49°. When this was refused by Great Britain, he did, it is true, adopt in public a somewhat truculent tone, but he did not have the support of influential members of his own party in a militant policy, and he could not fail to be hampered by the developing crisis with Mexico. As for the British, despite the tactless tone in which the President's offer was rejected, they had no stomach for a possible war. The Aberdeen ministry was not in general bellicose in temper; the 'outs,' the Whigs, whom a cabinet crisis presented with an opportunity for power at the end of 1845, were unable to form a ministry precisely because many of them did not wish to see the bellicose Palmerston at the Foreign Office; British economic interests in the region were confined to the fur-trade, which was almost finished; and the great debate over the repeal of the corn laws still further weakened the position of the Government. Despite the blood-and-thunder tone of a part of the American press, despite Polk's own bluster, despite the clamor in Congress for the denunciation of the agreement of joint occupation and the actual passage of a bill that carried out this purpose, matters turned out peaceably enough. When in June 1846 Aberdeen again proposed the line of 49° as far as Vancouver Island, the President yielded to the sentiment of his cabinet and, adopting a procedure that had hardly been used since the days of Washington, asked the Senate for its previous advice on a treaty embodying these terms. After two days' debate the Senate advised acceptance; a treaty was speedily drawn up and ratified, the more easily, no doubt, since the United States was now at war with Mexico. Thus the United States rounded out its territorial domain, with the exception of a small region acquired from Mexico in 1854, by which the way was cleared for a projected railway line through the Southwest to the Pacific. To complete the story of American continental acquisition, it is well to call attention also to the purchase of Alaska from Russia in 1867.

Such is the story of American expansion. There lies behind it, undeniably, a kind of land-hunger that unkind critics might suggest bears some analogy to the forces that set in motion the growth of modern Russia. That it involved only one war and a less amount of violence than is usually associated with territorial aggrandizement is due not so much to the morality of the Americans as to the fact that they occupied a sparsely settled continent. It is important to notice, however, that as matters stood in 1854, the process of growth had not led to the acquisition of territory containing important unassimilable elements. Signs of imperialism, in the sense of dominion over other peoples, there had been. The all-Mexico-or-none movement was an example. There was a hunger for Cuba in the eighteen-fifties, especially on the part of the South, which might conceivably have been satisfied had it not been for the appearance of the slavery issue and the opposition of Northerners to further expansion in the interests of the slave system. There was unofficial imperialism, like the famous filibustering expedition of William Walker, which resulted in this curious adventurer's setting himself up for a short time as the President of Nicaragua. But in no case did any area actually acquired in this period need to be governed as a dependency; it was easily brought within the political system of the United States and made a part of the Union. An immensely strong nation grew out of the process we have been examining.

A strong nation, but a provincial nation. American preoccupation with the problems of the American continent fostered and consolidated the spirit of isolationism. And this spirit was not without profound effects upon the diplomatic history of the United States.

III   AMERICAN ISOLATIONISM

In the first hundred years and more of the history of American foreign policy the distinctive feature, outside of the expansion of territory, is the crystallization of the tradition of what has come to be called isolationism. The two broad lines of tendency are connected, for it is precisely because the United States looked westward and southward to the increase of its dominion that it could and did in large degree, and increasingly, neglect the European scene. It was only after 1900, with the wider horizons that came with the Spanish-American War and the growth of American imperialism, that the scene changed and the story became more complex. To trace the growth of the isolationist point of view is essential to an understanding of American diplomacy.

The breach with Great Britain itself was, in a sense, an expression of the isolationist spirit. In his famous pamphlet, *Common Sense*, Thomas Paine, among other arguments, stressed the fact that an independent nation would not need always to be involved in Britain's wars, and that there was something absurd in the American continent's being governed by a distant island. True, it was one thing to assert this principle and another thing to pursue a truly independent course. Even in the early days of the Revolution the colonies depended much upon foreign aid, specifically French aid, and the greater part of the gunpowder with which the war was fought came, in default of adequate domestic manufacture, from across the seas. True, too, in 1778 the colonies entered into a full-fledged alliance with the French, and it was through the operation of this alliance that the decisive victory of Yorktown was won. Without the victory of the French fleet over the English, without the French troops of Rochambeau, which actually outnumbered the troops of the Continental line, the siege of Cornwallis's army and his final capitulation would never have occurred.

Yet the French alliance, even in so critical a period, was entered into reluctantly, and in its instructions to Benjamin Franklin in France, the Continental Congress could never bring itself to pronounce the decisive word. Moreover, when it came to the making of peace, as we have already seen, there was much suspicion of the French and a pronounced unwillingness to give them complete American confidence. France had committed herself to Spain as well as to the colonies, and in such circumstances the attitude of Adams and Jay must be considered as by no means completely unjustified. At Paris the first-named of these two men made to one of the British negotiators a classical statement of the isolationist point of view.

'"You are afraid," says Mr. Oswald today [writes Adams in his *Diary*] "of being made the tools of the powers of Europe." "Indeed I am," says I. "What powers?" said he. "All of them," said I. "It is obvious that all the powers of Europe will be continually maneuvering with us, to work us into their real or imaginary balances of power. They will all wish to make of us a make-weight candle. But, I think it ought to be our rule not to meddle."'

This statement is typical of many others. Before the Constitution was framed, John Jay, Secretary of State under the preceding government, made an effort to extricate the United States from the French alliance (which had no limit of time), and in the drafting of the Constitution the two-thirds rule with treaties and the prohibition against the acceptance of foreign honors both reflect the fear of entanglement. Moreover, when the French revolutionary wars broke out, and when Britain entered the struggle in the winter of 1793, the administration of General Washington from the first was determined on neutrality. It is a common misconception that, in the cabinet of the first President, Jefferson took one position and Hamilton another on the basic issue. This was not the case. The two great rivals differed in detail, not on principle. Neither wished to see the United States obliged to go to war on the side of the French.

There can be little doubt that, in the circumstances, neutrality was the wise course. The country was much divided in opinion, and, in the first days of its nationhood, it would have been risky for it to take sides, dangerous to its national integrity, in fact. It had a meager army and no navy whatsoever. It needed peace to consolidate the financial structure that had been built by the genius of Hamilton. As an exporter of foodstuffs, it was bound to profit from neutrality, a truth that Jefferson pungently phrased when he declared that now that the war had come 'we have only to pray that their soldiers may eat a great deal.'

But neutrality, it must be confessed, was easier to defend in theory than to carry out in practice. In this as in every subsequent general European war since the birth of the nation, the people of the United States were not able to preserve that judicial detachment, that cold objectivity, on which neutrality is best based. Party passions ran high between the friends of France and the friends of England, and what appeared to one group ignoble surrender appeared to the other group as judicious statesmanship. This was well illustrated by the famous Jay treaty of 1794 with Great Britain. The treaty secured from the British surrender of the border posts on the Lakes, which they had engaged to give up under the treaty of 1783; it gave the United States certain commercial advantages and provided for the peaceful arbitration of numerous disputed questions; but it made great concessions to the British with regard to the rights of neutrals on the sea and came close to violating, if not the letter, at least the spirit, of the treaty of alliance with France. It was hotly defended by the friends of England, the conservative elements in the country, and as hotly attacked by the friends of France. Few issues aroused a more intense popular passion.

The Jay treaty, moreover, had its troublesome sequel. It may have helped in the settlement of the dispute with Spain and facilitated the negotiation of Pinckney's treaty, alluded to in the preceding chapter; but it infuriated the French, led to renewed efforts on their part to strike down American commerce with England, and afforded an excuse, one cannot call it a justification, for the shameless interference of the French minister in the internal and domestic affairs of the United States. Much disturbed by all these facts, George Washington, before his departure from office, determined to read the American people a lesson on foreign, and also on domestic, policy, and the result was the famous Farewell Address of 19 September 1796. The part of this Address that deals with foreign relations has not always been fully understood. Washington's first injunction ran in these terms: 'Nothing is more essential than that permament, inveterate antipathies against particular nations and passionate attachments for others should be excluded. . . . The nation which indulges toward another an habitual hatred or an habitual fondness is in some degree a slave.' There is here a truth that is as sound today as when it was first enunciated. It has nothing to do with alliances, or the lack of alliances. It merely says that a nation should not be deflected from the course of its own interest by an emotional preference or hostility. When it came to the question of alliances, the President did not take quite the tone that some of our later isolationists have wished to attribute to him. He *did* write as follows: 'Why forego the advantages of so peculiar a situation? [i.e., as ours] Why quit our own to stand upon foreign ground? Why . . . entangle our peace and prosperity in the toils of European ambition, rivalship, interest, humor, or caprice?' But he did not exclude the possibility of association with another power. 'It is our true policy', he wrote, 'to steer clear of *permanent* alliances with any portion of the foreign world.' But 'we may safely trust to *temporary* alliances for extraordinary emergencies.' (The italics are mine.)

Notwithstanding this guarded and qualified language, it must be confessed that the general tone of the Farewell Address is what today would be called isolationist, and it was long to furnish an authoritative support to the isolationist point of view. Furthermore, there can be no question that Washington was much influenced by the irksomeness of the engagements that the United States had taken with regard to France, and was deducing his general point of view from this specific theme. As for the French, on their side, they never treated the American government with greater contempt than in the period just following 1796. The American envoy sent to Paris was denied a reception; and, when John Adams sent a tripartite mission a little later, its members were not only told that they must grease the palms of the French foreign minister, but also that they could buy immunity from French depredations of the sea only by a virtual forced loan to the Directory. The result of these demands was an outburst of indignation in the United States; an informal war with France was waged in 1798 and 1799; it offered a pretext for the denunciation of the treaty of alliance of 6 February 1778. When peace was made in 1800, the alliance was not renewed; and thus the American government was freed of the only compact of this kind it ever made until more than a century and two score years later.

Yet it is only right to say that American statesmen played with the idea of association with some European power for some years after the Farewell Address and after the war with France. There were Federalists, for example, of whom Alexander Hamilton was one, who were willing to draw close to England in 1798 and 1799, to combine in war against France, and to plunder France's ally, Spain, of some of her colonial possessions. A few years later, Thomas Jefferson, as we have seen, was ready to come to an understanding with Britain if France installed herself at New Orleans; in fact, in his famous mission to France, Monroe was instructed to cross the channel and seek an alliance with the British government if his negotiations failed; and Jefferson again played with the idea of an Anglo-American combination in connection with the Florida question. At a much later date, as we shall see, the possibility of the joint action of the two great English-speaking states was mooted in connection with the events leading up to the Monroe Doctrine. But the general drift of American policy was more and more in the direction of aloofness from Europe, and this tendency was accentuated by the events of the first quarter of the nineteenth century. The philosopher of Monticello, in his inaugural, gave new currency to the idea of isolation with his famous phrase, 'Peace, commerce and honest friendship with all nations, entangling alliances with none,' and, in general, the events of his administration reinforced this maxim. The purchase of Louisiana, for example, by reducing the amount of territory on the North American continent not in American hands and opening up a vast area for future expansion in the West, intensified the American or Continental view; and it is a fact of great significance that, confronted by the violation of American rights on the high seas by the European belligerents in the Napoleonic wars, Jefferson and his party supporters turned to the weapon of the embargo. A prohibition on trade with belligerents as a means of bringing them to respect American rights was based on the idea of withdrawal from the Old World, as if in a kind of sulky distaste for its methods and policies; and perhaps it is more important to note this fact than the fact that the embargo itself failed, as a result of the tremendous internal stresses it generated in the United States. In the same way, it is significant that, when the country finally went to war with Great Britain in 1812, it entered into no alliance with Britain's secular enemy, France. It fought a war of its own, unrelated to the European struggle, a war (it may be said incidentally) that was heartily disliked by large sections of American opinion, especially in New England, and, by the discontents that it aroused, underlined the danger to national unity that might lie in any involvement with the powers of Europe.

In the decade following the War of 1812, events carried the United States further along the isolationist course. During the Napoleonic struggle the Spanish American colonies began their revolution against Spain; and this fact was striking evidence of the separation of the New World from the Old. Brazil, too, was to become independent; and by 1825, of the vast colonial dominions that existed at the time of the adoption of the Constitution, only the islands of the Caribbean (except Santo Domingo) and the three Guianas, on the coast of South America, remained.

It was in connection with the revolt of the Spanish colonies that the United States had occasion to enunciate the famous principle that came to be known as the Monroe Doctrine, and that was a new assertion of the divergent destinies of the New World and the Old. From the outset, the American government had followed the colonial risings with sympathy; there was a tendency, sometimes carried to an extreme, to compare the revolutions in Latin America to that which had taken place in the United States; and while Europe, sinking into reaction after the Napoleonic wars, viewed with increasing distaste the course of events in America, the judgment of most Americans on the same events was a favorable one. In 1822, in an act whose boldness deserves to be emphasized, the American government recognized the independence of the colonies in defiance of the opinion of Continental Europe; and in 1823 it proceeded to a step that was still more significant, and whose origins must be carefully examined.

The powers of continental Europe, in the years following the peace of 1815, arrogated to themselves more and more as time went on the right to snuff out the flames of liberalism and of revolution. In 1821 they intervened in Naples to put down a movement for constitutional monarchy, and in 1822 they made France their agent to crush the Spanish movement of the same kind and to restore Ferdinand VII, one of the most worthless of sovereigns, to absolute rule. In the summer of 1823 there seemed to be some likelihood that the next step would be to call a Congress to discuss the affairs of Latin America and conceivably to plan some action against the newborn states of the New World. News of these designs was communicated to Richard Rush, our minister in London, by George Canning, the British Foreign Secretary, in August 1823. The British minister even went so far as to propose a joint declaration on the part of the United States and Great Britain on the subject of the colonies. Rush, able man that he was, refused to commit himself without referring the matter to Washington. There his dispatches, combined with the somewhat troubling language of the Tsar, produced the fear that ambitious projects of force might be in the wind. What was to be done? And how? Was the United States to speak out or not? If it did speak out, was it to associate itself with Great Britain or was it to act independently? These momentous questions were warmly discussed in the cabinet meetings of the fall of 1823. They were also the subject of a special correspondence carried on by President Monroe with his two predecessors, Jefferson and Madison. Both of these venerable men inclined to the acceptance of the British invitation. Joint action, in an interest so clearly American, had no terrors for them. But John Quincy Adams, the Secretary of State, took a different view. He was not minded that the United States should 'come in as a cockboat in the wake of the British man-of-war.' As for the President, though he had no objection to joint action, he was willing for the United States to go in advance of the British and act independently. Thus the message to Congress of 2 December 1823 served solemn notice on the Old World that the United States could not view any interposition on the part of Old World states 'for the purpose of oppressing' or of 'controlling in any other manner' the destiny of the new republics 'in any other light than as the manifestation of an unfriendly disposition toward the United States,' and as 'dangerous to our peace and safety.' In its tone, moreover, the President's warning drew a clear line between the two hemispheres, declaring categorically that the political system of the United States was essentially different from that of the allied powers, and that extension of that system to this hemisphere was to be viewed only with apprehension. And, to cap all this, there was incorporated in the message of 1823 an allusion to the controversy with Russia over the northwest coast and the disputed region between the 42nd parallel and the 54th, in which it was declared that 'the American continents, by the free and independent condition which they have assumed and maintain, are henceforth not to be considered as subjects for future colonization by any European powers.' This declaration, bold and forthright as it was, and none too easy to justify on grounds of international law, was surely one of the most extraordinary expressions of the gulf between the New World and the Old that ever came from the pen of an American statesman.

We must not exaggerate the immediate effects of the message of 1823. The danger of the Spanish American colonies from the powers of the Old World we now know was illusory; the American government hedged remarkably when some of the Latin American states tried to translate it into a more binding commitment; and the opposition to turning the presidential declaration into an international engagement was vigorously expressed in Congress in the debates of two years later. Moreover, the prohibition on European colonization was never accepted by Russia, and it was soon challenged by Great Britain. But looking at the matter more broadly we may say that, except for the Farewell Address, no pronouncement made by an American statesman was ever more influential. There was here foreshadowed a sense of the solidarity of the American states that was later to take form in Pan-Americanism; and there was here forged a principle that gave to the most remote New World republic (and such states as Argentina and Chile were remote, indeed, far more remote than Britain or France) a peculiar association with the United States.

It took time for the Monroe message to grow into doctrine. It was hardly applied at all for nearly two decades after its original enunciation; and, when it underwent a revival in the administration of President Polk (who had opposed it, at least in spirit, in the Congress of 1826), it was at first rather a doctrine of the Democratic party than of the nation as a whole. Yet, in the late eighteen-forties and early 'fifties, it became more definite in its form; it was invoked again and again in the controversy that arose with Great Britain with regard to British pretensions in Central America; and it was described as Doctrine as early, at least, as 1853. There was a distinct tendency to regard it as a national shibboleth before the 'fifties were over.

But what gave the Doctrine a very wide acceptance was the French attempt to set up a monarchy in Mexico in the period of the Civil War. The Emperor Napoleon III, anxious to curry favor with the Catholics at home and to take advantage of the internecine conflict in America to erect a barrier against American expansion, launched upon an intervention in the distraught Republic to the south that culminated in the establishment of a monarchy, and in the selection of an Austrian Archduke to occupy the Mexican throne. This enterprise was naturally regarded with intense dislike in Washington. During the Civil War it was, of course, impossible to do anything about the matter; Secretary Seward could only keep the record open by frequent appeals to the spirit of the message of 1823; but when the war was over American public opinion made itself felt in no uncertain fashion. Though the administration made no direct citation of the Doctrine in its diplomatic correspondence, there was plenty of appeal to it in the American press and by American public figures; and the pressure applied to the French government to withdraw its troops from Mexico was stepped up in one diplomatic communication after another until the Emperor of the French capitulated. We must not assume that his action was due to the attitude of the United States alone; the gallant resistance of the Mexicans themselves was a cardinal factor; while the opposition to the venture by the French liberals, the enormous expense of the enterprise, and the rise of German power in Europe, all contributed to the final result. But the final downfall of Maximilian's regime was connected with the acceptance by the American people, to a degree never before realized, of the principles of 1823; and, after the eighteen-sixties, it is fair to say that the Monroe Doctrine long went unchallenged by any European power. The concept of a New World dedicated to republicanism and democracy and different from the Old, became with time less correspondent with reality; certainly, as the nineteenth century lengthened, there were European states more truly imbued with the republican or, at any rate, the democratic spirit than some of those of Latin America; but the sense of differentness persisted; and from that day to this it has always been possible to appeal to the American people on the basis of the Monroe Doctrine, and on the assumption of a certain kinship between the states of the American continent. The notion of the two spheres cut deep into the American mind and has more than once influenced the practical evolution of American diplomacy.

There were some interesting practical expressions of this spirit in the succeeding period. For example, in the eighteen-fifties the United States had been willing to enter into a compact for the joint control of an inter-oceanic canal; but, when at the end of the 'seventies, the French entered the field with an actual effort to construct such a canal there was much concern, and President Hayes laid down the principle, deduced from the Monroe Doctrine, that any such waterway ought to be under the control of his own country. More extraordinary still, and less logical, was the position taken by Grover Cleveland in 1895 that when a European state—in the specific case, Great Britain—was involved in a boundary controversy with an American state—in the specific case, Venezuela—over American territory, it must submit its dispute to arbitration or suffer the American government to determine the result. Cleveland's stand in this instance was received with immense applause at the time; and, though the final solution of the controversy took some account of the position of Great Britain, it demonstrated how powerful was the appeal of the great diplomatic dogma laid down by President Monroe more than seventy years earlier.

Also, as we shall see, when a few years later the United States embarked upon a more adventurous career, and the annexation of territory in the Orient, the Doctrine was again and again cited as a strong argument against this new course of action, and it was argued by more than one American statesman that, if the Americans were to file a caveat on European action in the New World, it behooved them to keep out of other preserves. While this position was not maintained, while, on the contrary, the thesis began to be put forward that because the United States had special interests in the American hemisphere it could not be said to have no interests at all elsewhere, the gradual acceptance of this point of view was rather a sign of the decline of the isolationist spirit with which the Doctrine had been associated than a renunciation of the Doctrine itself. As it expanded in power and influence, the American government was able at one and the same time to sustain the principle of the separateness of the New World and the efficacy of its own diplomatic action in a larger sphere.

In the nineteenth century there was little disposition to interfere in Europe or in Asia, in the political sense. The people of the United States never hesitated to express their sympathy with republicanism and liberty when it raised its head across seas; they became, for example, the ardent partisans of the Greeks in the eighteen-twenties; Monroe, indeed, had wished to recognize the Greek state at the time of the debates on his great message, until dissuaded by Adams, who believed that the administration should 'make an American cause and . . . adhere inflexibly to that'; there was instant recognition of the Second French Republic when it was established in 1848; there was much enthusiasm for the Hungarian movement for liberty, and, after it had been suppressed by the armies of Austria and Russia, Kossuth, its great leader, was received with tremendous acclaim in the United States; and in the period after the Civil War there was a not unnatural interest in the Irish question, intensified by the large Irish emigration to the United States. It was not, perhaps, unnatural that the American people should so express themselves; and if some Americans were disposed to criticize these expressions of opinion as not the best of diplomatic manners and as both irritating and futile, it cannot be said that the critics were either very numerous or very influential. On the contrary (and the fact is one that deserves to be emphasized), we must expect such ebullitions of feeling as a normal accompaniment of the democratic spirit. In a land of free speech and a free press, in a country as secure as the United States has been, and among a people drawn from various racial strains, the temptation to capitalize on democratic principles has been too strong for politicians to resist; nor is there, as a matter of fact, any sign that the situation has been fundamentally changed, even at the present day, though there may be perhaps a little more caution in the manner of expressing these points of view. Certainly in the nineteenth century the American people found no inconsistency between political isolation and the manifestation of their sympathies with those who suffered from what, to their eyes, was oppression and the violation of the principles of democracy.

They were, in fact, in this period, with regard to the rest of the world, remarkably naïve. Only a small educated class realized the degree to which democratic institutions had established themselves in Britain and in many other parts of Europe. The long peace that the Old World had enjoyed in the nineteenth century, or, to put it more exactly, the freedom from a general war, seemed to large numbers of Americans the harbinger of a new era. Until the eighteen-eighties the Americans can hardly be said to have had a modern navy, and, even at the end of a century, they lacked an army of substantial size. Though the passage of the years had brought them nearer to Europe in the temporal sense, though more and more travelers from the States trod the soil of the Old World, there was little realization of how intimately the events that took place in Europe might affect the United States. After all, almost a hundred years had elapsed since the wars of Napoleon, and, in that long period, it had hardly been necessary to reckon in any important way with the devious politics of the European chancelleries. Great Britain was an American power. Yet, in the years since the end of the War of 1812, every controversy with the British had been peaceably settled. Every foot of the boundary between Canada and the United States had been peaceably determined by arbitration or negotiation. Every subject of dispute with the Mistress of the Seas had concerned the New and not the Old World and had reinforced the sentiment of aloofness from Europe. In circumstances such as these, it is not strange that the Americans were a provincial people, hardly aware of the vast stage on which they might soon be called to play a part, and uninstructed in their view of what was happening there. The course of their national development could hardly have made them otherwise. And the mingling of many strains in their own land could hardly fail to convince them of the value and the possibility of peace.

Economically, too, they could afford, during most of the period we have been traversing, to be isolationist. Their high protective tariff was the expression of their immense self-sufficiency, of the tremendously varied possibilities of development that their country offered. Their foreign trade, though important, was only a fraction of their total economic activity. They were, until the last twenty years of the century, a country into which capital flowed rather than one from which it was exported. Their range was limited by the colossal success of their experiment in capitalism and by the hopes that that experiment inspired.

Yet the picture, as we shall see, was changing. It was changing by imperceptible degrees in the eighteen-eighties and the early 'nineties. There were new forces at work. These forces were to find expression in the war of 1898. They were to usher in a new period at that time. The United States as a world power dates from the days of William McKinley and from the new consciousness of strength and of purpose that was awakened in the struggle with Spain. To this new era we must now turn.

IV   AMERICAN IMPERIALISM

THERE can be little question that the year 1898 is a landmark in the development of American foreign policy. Not that any date can be truly decisive, or that it is possible, from the scholar's point of view, to cut the seamless web of history in two according to the calendar. Yet, roughly, it can be said that up to 1898 the United States looked inward; after 1898 she looked outward. It is unnecessary to emphasize the tremendous significance of this fact.

A Marxian would have a very easy explanation of this phenomenon. He would say that American capitalism had reached the point of saturation so far as the domestic market was concerned, and that by the inexorable laws of the capitalist order the business interests of the United States began to look for other worlds to conquer. Certainly, in the period to be examined in the following chapters, there are signs of such a phenomenon. America became in the twentieth century a capital-exporting nation—in Latin America, in the Orient, and with the loans of the 'twenties, even in Europe. Yet this fact, strange as it may appear, had less effect upon American foreign policy than outside observers are likely to assume. In a land of free enterprise, the foreign policy of business and of government were by no means always closely articulated. Such regimes as those of Woodrow Wilson and of Franklin Roosevelt had a character somewhat hostile to large economic interests. Even under more favorable circumstances, any appearance of truckling to 'Wall Street' often awakened unfavorable reactions in large parts of the country. A policy of all-out support for American investors in foreign lands was, at no time, very popular, and has rarely been carried through in practice. While it would be absurd to state that private economic interests have never affected public policy, though on matters of detail they not infrequently have done so, it would be still more absurd to

39

undertake to study the period upon which we are about to enter with the prepossessions of Marxist philosophy. Neat formulas in regard to the cause of human action are likely to be too tidy to be true; and economic determinism applied to American foreign policy is a case in point.

If we turn to the first important episode in the shifting scene of American diplomacy, that is, the Spanish-American War, we can illustrate the generalization we have been making. There were already important sugar interests in Cuba in 1898 when the United States took up the cudgels for Cuban independence. But these interests were by no means united in desiring American intervention; some at least were opposed to such action. On the contrary, the action of the American government is to be traced not to economic pressure, but to a change in the national mood.

These changes in national mood are a national phenomenon observable not only in the history of the United States but in the history of many other nations. There is a kind of rhythm in human action that baffles analysis, but that is a readily observable fact. The pacific and the bellicose temper, the mood of expansion and the mood of *recueillement*, follow one another again and again in the evolution of nations. In the long period after the Civil War the United States was on the whole extremely conservative in its outlook on foreign affairs. But with the eighteen-nineties a new generation had grown to manhood, a generation to whom the bitter bloodshed of the Civil War was only a glorious memory. A new and confident nationalism began to express itself. It was typified in politics by such men as Lodge and the youthful Theodore Roosevelt. It was typified in the navy by the writings of Alfred Thayer Mahan, perhaps the most influential of American publicists, with his emphasis on the role of sea power. It was typified in the university by men like Burgess, with his avowed doctrine of the superiority of the so-called Nordic peoples. It was typified in religion by men like Josiah Strong, with his preachments of enlarged national duty. And it was soon to be translated into national policy in the administration of William McKinley.

It is not strange that this new mood expressed itself most strikingly, and, as events were to demonstrate, most significantly, with regard to Cuba. Cuba had long been an interest of the United States, as we have seen, even before the Civil War. In the course of the revolt that began in 1868, also, American opinion had been by no means indifferent. And when once again revolution broke forth in 1895, public sentiment was easy to arouse. Grover Cleveland, President at the time, opposed any provocative action against Spain with all the granite obstinacy of his powerful will, but in the elections of 1896 the Republican party declared for the independence of Cuba; and William McKinley, who assumed the presidency in March 1897, though pacific by temperament, was by no means a man to resist to the last the gathering tide of public opinion. The administration began, it is true, with moderate conceptions of policy, but it found public sentiment by no means calm. In New York City a tremendous newspaper duel was raging between Joseph Pulitzer and the young William Randolph Hearst, and, as each found new factors to dramatize in the Cuban struggle, excitement naturally rose to greater and greater heights. Public excitement was further fanned by the publication of a dispatch by the Spanish minister at Washington, in which he spoke depreciatingly of the President, and, to an infinitely greater extent, by the explosion on the American battleship *Maine*, in the harbor of Havana, with the loss of the vessel and a great part of its crew. The administration stepped up its tone with regard to Spain; the hardpressed Spanish Government, forced to concession, conceded too late; McKinley failed to stress its concessions to an inflamed Congress, and in April came war. Never was there a clearer case of a war brought about by public opinion, rather than by special interests; American businessmen were, on the whole, by no means enthusiastic about intervention; it was the newspapers and the people who demanded action. It is sometimes said that the President could have forestalled both if he had emphasized more positively the last pacific gestures of Spain; but it seems almost equally probable that the Cuban insurgents would, in any case, have refused to treat with the mother country and would have forced the American action from which they stood to gain.

At any rate, war came. We shall treat of its Oriental aspects and of the conquest of the Philippines in a later chapter. So far as Cuba was concerned, it naturally ended in the expulsion of the Spaniards and in the overrunning by the United States of the island of Puerto Rico. It left the United States in the Caribbean, no less than in the Orient, in possession of territories that could not be admitted into the Union and that inevitably suggested the practice of a type of imperialism.

The decision to embark upon this new course of action was warmly debated by the American people. To many distinguished statesmen, such as George Frisbie Hoar, senior Senator from Massachusetts, the decision to acquire and govern dependent regions was a dangerous breach with the past, a violation of American ideals, an invitation to involvement in world affairs, and an assumption of undesirable world responsibilities. The treaty of peace with Spain was ratified in the Senate by the narrow margin of 57 to 27 (one more than the necessary two-thirds), and then only through the intervention of William Jennings Bryan, the titular leader of the Democratic party, and perhaps because of the bursting out of a revolt in the Philippines against the American forces of occupation, which made it difficult to 'haul down the flag.' Like so many important decisions in the field of American foreign policy, this one was adopted only after a violent partisan debate, in which no doubt both honest conviction and partisan tactics played a part. But adopted, none the less, it was; and it seemed to be confirmed by the triumphant re-election of President McKinley in the campaign of 1900.

The temper that produced the Spanish-American War was to have far-reaching consequences. It was typified, as chance would have it, in the person of Theodore Roosevelt, who moved from the vice-presidency into the presidency on the assassination of McKinley in the fall of 1901. This amazing man, vigorous, self-confident, a natural regulator of others, approached world affairs in a positive and militant spirit. The war had changed the position of the United States in the Caribbean and given it important new strategic interests there. What followed was in the circumstances wholly natural.

Among other things, the struggle with Spain had underlined the necessity of easier communication between the east and west coasts of the United States, in other words, had given a new impetus to the movement for an inter-oceanic canal. Such a canal had been for some time projected, and as early as 1850 the United States and Great Britain had signed a treaty providing for the joint control of such a waterway. But the United States had grown increasingly restive at this bargain, and in 1900 the British, anxious for American friendship, conceded in the Hay-Pauncefote treaty exclusive rights to the United States. It remained, then, to make a compact with either Colombia, which controlled the Panama route, or with Nicaragua for the actual construction of the waterway. The course Roosevelt followed in this matter has been the subject of much criticism. He was the partisan of the Panama route; and in 1902 a treaty with Colombia, the owner of the Isthmian territory, was negotiated. But at Bogotá this treaty was by no means well received in the Colombian Congress, and when it came to a vote it was defeated. Much enraged (as much enraged as some foreigners have been from time to time at the action of the American Senate), Roosevelt first thought of forcibly undertaking the construction of the canal, and even got from an eminent source a legalistic justification of such a course based on an old treaty. But an alternative presented itself. There were special interests involved in the matter, the interests of a former canal company chartered in France, the interests of the Panamanians who stood to gain from the building of the waterway. These interests plotted a revolution and contrived to let Roosevelt know of what was in the wind. When the decisive moment for action arrived, therefore, American vessels were in the neighborhood; American marines were landed; and the Colombian troops on the spot, succumbing to a mixture of intimidation and bribery, were persuaded to renounce any attempt at suppression of the revolt and to sail away. There followed the hasty recognition of the new government at Panama, the negotiation of a treaty, and its prompt ratification by the Senate of the United States. The United States had not actually instigated the revolution; its agents advanced no funds to the revolutionists nor did they grease the palms of the Colombians, but Roosevelt's later candid comment that he 'took Panama' expressed the view that was widely held by his critics. At any rate, here was a new area of American influence; here was a new state that might, in these early days, be not inaccurately described as a protectorate of the Americans.

There were other respects in which the Roosevelt period was a period of expanding American influence over the countries of the Caribbean. The United States withdrew from Cuba in 1902, but only after compelling the Cubans to agree, in what became known as the Platt Amendment, to an American right of intervention 'for the purpose of preserving order and maintaining Cuban independence,' acquiring a naval base in the island, and binding the Cuban government not to incur too large an indebtedness. American troops were in the island again in 1906 and remained there until 1909 (though it is only fair to say that in this case the administration acted most reluctantly).

More important was the new twist that Roosevelt gave to the Monroe Doctrine. American opinion had been much roused by the chastisement of a miserable little Venezuelan dictator, Cipriano Castro, by a combined Anglo-German-Italian force in 1902, and especially by a blockade of the Venezuelan coast. The incident was ended without an actual international explosion. But it set the President to thinking about the future and about the dangers incident to European intervention ostensibly for the vindication of just claims, but directed (possibly at any rate) toward the occupation of American territory. Such an occupation could be dangerous, especially in the Caribbean. Partly at the suggestion of the British, the militant Theodore in 1904 laid down a new principle, namely, that 'chronic wrong-doing may in America as elsewhere, ultimately require intervention by some civilized nation, and in the Western hemisphere the adherence of the United States to the Monroe Doctrine may force the United States, however reluctantly, in flagrant case of wrong doing or impotence to the exercise of an international police power.'

The first opportunity to apply this maxim came in the case of the Dominican Republic. This little state had been sore beset by revolution; it had many European creditors. In order to keep it out of trouble, President Roosevelt perhaps instigated, and certainly engineered, an arrangement by which the customs houses were brought under American control; and, when the Senate refused to ratify a treaty regularizing this arrangement, he sent vessels to the coast of the Republic to prevent new revolutionary outbreaks, and carried out his policy by means of an executive agreement (that is, a mere understanding between the American and the Dominican administrations). Perhaps, strictly speaking, this was not intervention; but it paved the way for what *was* intervention in the future. For under the two succeeding administrations, actual armed interference did take place. Secretary Knox, Taft's Secretary of State, was a strong believer in the Roosevelt corollary. He engineered agreements with Nicaragua and Honduras similar to that which had been arranged with the Dominican Republic; the latter of these was never carried into effect; but in the case of Nicaragua, matters fell out in such fashion as brought about the landing of American marines. The regime with which the treaty was negotiated was threatened with revolution; advances had been made to it by American bankers at the request of the State Department; and, in order to protect its position with regard to these same bankers, the administration found it necessary to intervene. Let no one describe this as 'financial imperialism'; the financial interests acted at the solicitation of the Government, rather than on their own initiative; and Knox's own motives were, like those of Roosevelt before him, more concerned with limiting European influence in an area where American strategic interests were important than with securing a profit for American businessmen. Indeed, the State Department was oftentimes completely dissociated from the unofficial imperialism of the fruit companies. In the years between 1900 and 1912 these companies made and unmade Central American governments, even fomenting revolution to serve their selfish interests.

The intervention in Nicaragua that took place in 1912 was followed by two others in the administration of Woodrow Wilson. It seems strange that this ardent apostle of democracy and self-determination should so act, or that his Secretary of State, Bryan, should be associated with him in one of these two interventions. But the regulatory spirit is strong in the virtuous, and certainly the two states concerned presented a rather striking case for regulation. Haiti, where American marines landed in the summer of 1915, had been in anarchy during most of the twentieth century; the State Department, under the influence, no doubt, of its professional personnel, attempted to negotiate an agreement for customs control on diverse occasions; successive Haitian Presidents evaded the issue; and, finally, a particularly outrageous revolution, in which the body of a former President was dismembered and paraded through the streets of Port-au-Prince, precipitated the landing of the marines. The Dominican Republic, too, after some years of tranquillity following on the agreement of 1905, became a prey to civil disturbance; and the resulting situation offered an excuse, if not a justification, for the occupation of the Republic. Thus, by the fall of 1916, American marines were encamped on the soil of three Caribbean states.

American techniques with regard to these interventions deserve a word of mention. On the political side, a different procedure was followed in each case. In Nicaragua the existing government was sustained, and the party to which it belonged afterwards kept in power. In Haiti the legislature was suppressed, but a President and a nominated Council of State were allowed to exist. In the Dominican Republic the national government was suppressed by the American military regime. In Nicaragua there was, except for a brief period toward the end of the occupation, little resistance to the Americans; but in Haiti and the Dominican Republic there was a savage outburst of guerrilla warfare, with its inevitable accompaniment of atrocities and demands for congressional investigation at home. In all three states much was done to restore financial good order; in

Haiti and to a lesser degree in the Dominican Republic there was an important road-building program; and in these two states, too, something was done for education. In Haiti there was also an ambitious and serviceable health program. Finally, in all three instances, a constabulary was created, which was thought to be in the future a sure preventive of revolutionary disturbance. One could be more enthusiastic over this last reform if, in practice, it had not in two instances resulted in the establishment of military dictatorships headed by the ambitious chiefs of this trained force, Somoza in Nicaragua, and Trujillo in the Dominican Republic.

The interventions that we have just mentioned lasted for varying periods of time. The Americans got out of the Dominican Republic in 1924; they left Nicaragua in 1925, but soon went back and stayed until 1932; they remained in Haiti until 1934. None of the occupations, in other words, extended over a period of as long as twenty years. Even their severest critic will not deny that they performed certain constructive services to the peoples whom they affected; and at the very least it may be said that there has been no chronic anarchy in any of these states since the Americans went in. It is to be noted that they lasted only a short time; that they were subjected to severe criticism in the United States; and that they were never popular with the American people as a whole. American imperialism, even in its most extreme form, can hardly be described as ruthless domination; and it is fair to say that the imperialist mood in American foreign policy was rather a passing phase of affairs than a deep-seated and passionately cherished sentiment. American imperialism, in fact, was always imperialism with an uneasy conscience; and the deep wellsprings of American democratic faith have made American rule, wherever extended, something different from the arrogant rule of a Hitler or a Mussolini.

The case of Mexico illustrates the divergence between governmental policy and private business interest, to which we briefly alluded at the beginning of this chapter. There were large investments in this rich and growing country in the late nineteenth and early twentieth century, investments amounting to over one billion dollars in 1912. American business concerns were, naturally, entirely happy so long as Porfirio Diaz, the handy-man of capitalism, occupied the center of the stage. But they were by no means so contented when a long overdue social and political revolution broke out in Mexico. With the unsettled conditions of 1911 and 1912, they began a clamor for intervention; nor did they hesitate, at times, to foment domestic strife and to defy the weak and distracted government of Francisco Madero. There is here a shoddy chapter in what we may describe as 'private imperialism.' But the attitude of the American government did not reflect this point of view.

At the moment of the revolutionary outbreak, the Taft administration was in power in the United States. Frequently denounced by its enemies as reactionary, one might have expected it to take a blustering or minatory tone or even to intervene to restore order. It did nothing of the kind. True, American troops were mobilized on the border; there was a rather sharp exchange of notes toward the end of 1912 when conditions in Mexico were still disturbed; but there was no other action, and President Taft scrupulously refrained from taking any step that might tie the hands of his successor.

The policy of Woodrow Wilson cannot be summed up so easily. The story must be told in some detail before judgment can be made. It begins with the revolutionary *coup d'état* that deposed Madero and brought Victoriano Huerto into power, almost at the same time that Wilson himself was assuming the presidency. The new regime undoubtedly represented stark reaction. Moreover, its advent was followed by the murder of Madero, probably at the orders of Huerta. Shocked at these events, Wilson declared at the outset of his administration that he would not recognize a government that had attained power by violence. In part, too, he was influenced by his fundamental sympathy with the revolution in Mexico, and his desire that the Mexican people should come into their own. With such motives, he was led into measures that certainly constituted interference in the affairs of Mexico. To withhold recognition from Huerta might have been justified on traditional grounds, for there was another regime in the north under General Carranza, and Huerta did not control the whole country; but in his desire to see the dictator fall from power, Wilson was led more and more to take sides. In the winter of 1914 he lifted the arms embargo on the shipment of arms into Mexico, clearly with a view to favoring the insurgents; and in April of the same year he took a still more decisive step. At the port of Tampico was an American squadron under Admiral Mayo. Members of the crew of a small boat attached to the squadron were arrested by a Mexican force that owed allegiance to Huerta. Though the Americans had been speedily released, the Admiral demanded an apology and a salute to the flag. Extreme though the demand was in the circumstances, Wilson backed him up. There was some diplomatic haggling; but on the morning of 21 April, influenced in part by the approach of a German vessel bearing arms for Huerta, the President gave the order for the seizure of the port of Vera Cruz. The Mexicans naturally resisted, and it looked as if the country were on the verge of war. In this serious situation, the ABC powers offered a way out by proposing mediation. The offer was gladly accepted. The Americans remained in Vera Cruz; and, while negotiations were carried on with the Mexican dictator, his power ebbed, since he could no longer get supplies. In the fall of 1915 General Carranza entered Mexico City.

But Wilson's troubles with Mexico were by no means over. The revolution entered upon a new phase. Revolt in the north broke out, and its leader, the ex-bandit, Francisco Villa, proceeded to harass the border, perhaps with a view to provoking intervention or in retaliation for the recognition of Carranza by the United States. On one occasion he sacked the American town of Columbus, New Mexico, leaving behind seventeen slain Americans. Unable to get much satisfaction from Carranza (a prickly and obstinate person at best), the American President directed General Pershing to cross the boundary and to capture Villa. The mission was a failure; and a clash with the Mexican troops at Carrizal again created a situation that might have meant war. But the President was determined that in no case would the United States embark upon a full intervention, and the incident of Carrizal, like the incident of Vera Cruz, was turned over to negotiation. With the entry of America into the First World War in April 1917, the Mexican question disappeared from the diplomatic foreground. The Mexicans drew up a new and radical Constitution, calling for the nationalization of Mexico's sub-soil resources of petroleum, for a program of agrarian reform, and for sharp measures of repression against the Church; and the Revolution entered upon a new phase, the consolidation of its position and the practical execution of its policies. There was a new agitation for intervention in 1920, fanned by certain American interests; but once again the administration made it clear that no such action would be taken.

As one reviews these years, one finds in the President's policy the note of moral imperialism. 'I want to teach the Latin-American republics to elect good men,' he is reported to have said to a British visitor. The note of superior virtue in this statement is, we may be sure, a little difficult for our southern neighbors to enjoy. Moreover, in his dislike of Huerta, the President was led perilously near to war.

Yet, despite these criticisms, one large fact stands out and deserves to be underlined. The President of the United States, in his Mexican policy, was not guided by the selfish American interests that clamored for intervention in Mexico. Not only did he not act to suppress, but in effect he encouraged a revolutionary movement that was certainly opposed to the interests of American capital. He held his hand when it would have been easy to bring about a war. His action was hardly such as we connect with imperialism, in the old-fashioned or political sense of the term.

The restraint shown by the United States in the case of Mexico goes a long way to offset the interference in the republics of the Caribbean. Nor must the American record in Cuba be forgotten. Here was an area into which American capital poured in substantial amounts after the Spanish-American War. It lay at the very doors of the United States. American interest in it could not fail to be keen. But in 1902, as we have seen, the American government redeemed the promise to give independence to Cuba, with mild reservations. Going in again in 1906, it got out in 1909. While it would be too much by far to say that after 1909 there was never diplomatic interference or diplomatic pressure, it is not often in the history of imperialism that we read of a powerful nation withdrawing from territory which it had occupied (except under threat of force), or leaving to those in whom it had an interest a greater degree of freedom in the working out of their own government. Even in the heyday of American imperialism, it will be seen, there are two sides to the coin.

Yet it must be conceded that, with the beginning of the twentieth century, there began an era in which the United States was by no means popular in Latin America. Its power, however used, was portentous. The note of superiority, sometimes of supercilious superiority, in some of its diplomatic utterances, was unmistakable. American statesmen were by no means always careful of Latin-American susceptibilities. And strive as Woodrow Wilson did to bring about a better attitude, he succeeded only in part. When in 1917 the World War came to the United States, the Caribbean states, with the exception of El Salvador, entered the struggle alongside the United States. But the greater states in the Latin American galaxy held aloof. Mexico was far from friendly, despite Wilsonian forbearance. Colombia was neutral, remembering Panama. So, too, was Venezuela. And so, too, were Argentina and Chile. Of the more powerful republics, only Brazil stood by the side of the Colossus of the North.

'The Colossus of the North.' In that phrase lay embodied the suspicions of the other nations of the New World. The United States was a formidable power. It often acted without consultation with its neighbors. True, its investments, particularly in the 'twenties, were expanding. But this expansion did not bring a cordial friendship in its train, despite more than one friendly gesture. Indeed, in the 'twenties, opposition to American 'imperialism' tended to grow rather than to diminish, and found its principal expression at the Pan-American Conferences.

These conferences, which were based upon the common interests of the American states, had begun, so far as the United States was concerned, with James G. Blaine, in 1889. Three more were held before the American entry into the Great War. But it was not until the Fifth Conference, at Santiago de Chile in 1923, that opposition to the United States began to manifest itself rather sharply. There, criticism was candid; and an attempt to remodel the machinery of the Pan American Union, which had its seat in Washington and was run by an American Director General, was brought forward. Moreover, a commission of jurists was appointed to codify American international law with a clear view to limiting the action of the United States. The years just following tended to make the issues more precise. After withdrawing from Nicaragua in 1925, the Coolidge administration sanctioned a new intervention there the next year. Moreover, by 1925, there was much tension in American relations with Mexico. The oil question, always troublesome, became acute with the attempt of the Mexican government to give a retroactive interpretation to the Constitution of 1917. At the same time the Mexican anticlerical program was highly offensive to many American Catholics. Nor did it help matters when the Secretary of State, Mr. Kellogg, yielding to an unfortunate impulse, identified the course of events in Mexico with Bolshevism. True, the situation took a turn for the better in 1927, with the dispatch of Dwight W. Morrow to the Mexican capital. But the resentment that had been aroused was not to be exorcised in a moment, and, when the Pan-American Conference met in Havana in 1928, the United States was certainly put on the spot. A determined effort was made to get adopted a resolution that would bar all intervention in the affairs of other states. To counter this movement, the administration called from retirement Charles Evans Hughes, one of the most respected figures in the country and Secretary of State from 1921 to 1925. With a lawyer's acumen and with a personal force peculiar to himself, Mr. Hughes tried to establish a distinction between what he called 'interposition' and intervention, but he did not make much headway. Clearly the majority of states at the Conference were aligned against the Americans. It was only after a very heated and a very frank debate that it was finally resolved to postpone the question until the meeting of the next Conference in 1933. The United States had been put on warning; what happened later we shall see shortly, in another chapter.

All in all, in the period from 1898 to 1928, it cannot be said that the growth of American power was fraught with profound menace to the other states of the New World. The instinct to domination was, no doubt, there; as we have seen, it found expression in some measure. But this is the halcyon period of American imperialism. As we look back upon it, we can see that the democratic tradition of the American people gave it a peculiar and distinctive flavor. It was the optimistic faith of the Americans that the peoples over whom they assumed control could be prepared for self-government. The idea of an enduring domination ran counter to their deepest instincts and to their national habits. When they went into Nicaragua, and Haiti, and the Dominican Republic, they went in with the implicit assumption that they would, in due course, deliver the power to a duly-elected government. This they had already done in the last-mentioned of these cases in 1924, and in Nicaragua by 1932.

Nor, even in this period, is there much evidence of economic domination, as distinguished from political control. In the Dominican Republic, administration was in some degree shaped to the encouragement of American interests. In Haiti, the law forbidding foreigners to own land was repealed. In Nicaragua, very little was attempted. If it is a sin to establish conditions of relative good order, in which capital can be invested in a country, then the Americans committed a sin. But the amounts of capital actually involved were meager, and it would be difficult to prove that they did harm. On the contrary, they tended, as prudent investment does tend, to raise the standard of living for at least a part of the population of the states concerned. To some minds, the terms capitalism and exploitation are synonymous. But how, one may fairly ask, is the world to make progress without capital? That it may be either private or public is conceded. But to get along without it is impossible.

None the less, it is not intended to close this chapter with an apologia. That the power of the United States, political and economic, should be distrusted was natural. That it was at times abused is certain. There was needed a newer and broader policy. That policy was to evolve, as we shall see in chapter VII.

V   THE EMERGING ORIENT

AMERICAN interest in the Orient goes back to the earliest days of national existence. Trade with China was begun before the Constitution was framed and was assuming substantial proportions by the beginning of the nineteenth century. But political relations were slow in developing, and the first diplomatic mission to the East, that of Roberts, was not sent out until the eighteen-thirties and touched at neither Japanese nor Chinese ports. By 1844, following on the heels of Great Britain, which had forced open the door of trade in the famous Opium War, the United States had negotiated a trade treaty with China, and once again in 1858, taking advantage of the coercive action of others, in this case both France and England, it had enlarged its privileges in its intercourse with the Middle Kingdom. More important, in its consequences, was the role played by the American government in the opening of Japan. The expedition of Matthew Calbraith Perry, planned in 1852 and brought to a happy conclusion in 1854, is one of the most picturesque episodes in our history. Up to this time the Japanese had excluded all foreigners except the Dutch, and these last were permitted to trade only through a single port. Without firing a single shot, by a rare mixture of firmness and tact, Perry succeeded in persuading the Japanese to reverse the policy of centuries. We must not be romantic about this enterprise. Force was not used, but force was in the background. Perry came with an imposing squadron, made a demonstration of power, withdrew to let the Japanese think things over, and returned. He was assisted in his enterprise by the fact that the Japanese government itself was undergoing a period of internal stress, and that the issue of freer trade was presented at the psychological moment. None the less, there have been few more significant accomplishments than that of the American commodore.

The work he did was ably supplemented by our first diplomatic representative to Japan, Townsend Harris. With Harris it was persuasion, and persuasion alone, that won the victory. Without an American warship within a thousand miles, as he himself boasted, he greatly enlarged the concessions that had been made to Perry, and established commercial intercourse with Nippon on terms consistent with modern notions and with the interests of the United States.

In the period before the Civil War, moreover, the Americans began to develop an interest in Hawaii. American whaling vessels and American missionaries (an incongruous combination) were going to the Hawaiian archipelago in some numbers by the period of the 'twenties. Religious and commercial interests were curiously blended in the development of closer relations. The Hawaiians were Christianized and their institutions remodeled along lines laid down by the white proselytizers. At the same time there developed a sugar industry, and the sons of the ministers of God often turned to pursuits of a mundane character. The United States watched events in Hawaii with a jealous eye and, as early as 1842, made it clear that it would not permit the islands to fall into the hands of any other power. In 1853 a treaty of annexation was negotiated, but a Congress in which Southern interests played a very great role could hardly be expected to view with enthusiasm the addition of a Kanaka state to the American Union. Installed on the Pacific by the war of 1846-48, the Americans were beginning to cast their eyes upon the regions of the East with a new interest that was to grow still further with time.

There is not much that needs to be recorded in the story of our relations with the Orient in the years between the Civil War and the outbreak of the struggle with Spain. Yet there were signs of a more active interest. In 1872, for example, an enterprising naval commander made a treaty with some Samoan chieftains, looking to the establishment of a naval base in these remote islands, six thousand miles from San Francisco; and six years later a more solemn and formal agreement was negotiated by which the United States secured rights to use the harbor of Pago Pago. Though the average American can have concerned himself little with such matters, the American representatives on the spot soon found themselves involved in acute rivalry with the Germans and the British. Their controversies (in which the Germans played the more annoying role) were sufficiently heated to arouse the interests of the chancelleries themselves, and in

1889 what might have been a serious situation, with vessels of war of all three nations in the harbor of Apia, was perhaps averted only by a serious hurricane that destroyed the greater part of these armaments. A condominium was established, that is, a kind of three-power rule (a clear violation, of course, of American traditional policy), and this ingenious but clumsy arrangement endured for a decade. With the American victory over Spain, the problem of the Pacific assumed a new character; the Samoa Islands were partitioned; and the United States received the best of them, among these Tutuila with the harbor of Pago Pago.

The Spanish-American War also brought our relations with Hawaii to a culminating point. In 1875 a reciprocity treaty was negotiated with the monarchy, by which Hawaiian interests were bound more closely than ever to the United States. Politically, the first crisis came in 1893. By this time the whites were so numerous as hardly to relish being governed by others. In a sense, Hawaii is West Florida and Texas all over again. When the Hawaiian Queen, Liliuokalani, seemed about to overthrow the Constitution which had been forced upon her predecessor, with a view to enlarging her own power, the influential whites revolted and set up a republican government. They were certainly not discouraged in this course by the American minister at Honolulu, and the landing of American marines and their presence at a strategic point in the city was later alleged (not entirely without reason) to have measurably assisted the revolutionists, and to have exercised a persuasive influence upon the Queen, who abdicated.

The Cleveland administration, which came into power shortly after these events, was by no means happy about what had occurred and made a half-hearted attempt to persuade the revolutionaries to reinstate the Queen; but the new Government stood its ground, and Hawaii was an independent republic until 1898. Then, using the precedent of 1845, though adapting it to another type of case, Hawaii was annexed by joint resolution, and constituted not a state, but a territory of the Union.

As for our relations with China and Japan in the years we have been discussing, they were for the most part untroubled. The only issue that arose was the issue of immigration, and, on that question, a distinct revulsion of feeling took place. In 1868 the Burlingame treaty with China permitted unrestricted entry to the United States to the inhabitants of the Middle Kingdom, and it was not at the time condemned. But a formidable sentiment grew up on the West Coast in the next decade, and by 1880 President Hayes was obliged to negotiate with Peking an agreement that permitted the suspension of immigration. Needless to say, this treaty paved the way for virtual exclusion.

The events of 1898, to which we have already alluded in connection with Hawaii and Samoa, were, in the East, as in the Caribbean, the herald of a new era. We have already seen how the battle of Manila Bay awakened in the American people not only a gratified pride but a new sense of interest in the Orient. These were the days when the nations of Europe were picking up bases and devising spheres of interest in disorganized China. The mere instinct to keep up with the Joneses would have dictated the acquisition of the islands. True, conservatives deeply deplored and bitterly fought the decision. But, as President McKinley stated, with somewhat unnecessary unctuousness but considerable cogency, we could not give them back to Spain, or permit them to be handed over to some other state; we were not, at the moment, in a mood to free them, or ready to believe that they could govern themselves; and the logic of the situation, therefore, called for their retention. Once installed there, the American position in the Far East was fundamentally altered. New responsibilities, both strategic and political, had been assumed by the United States.

That this change of position was sensed is demonstrated by the diplomacy of Secretary Hay and by the enunciation of the doctrine of the Open Door in China. In two famous notes, one dated 6 September 1899 and the other 3 July 1900, Hay laid down, first, the principle of non-discrimination and non-interference with vested interests, and, second, the principle of respect for the territorial integrity of China and of commercial equality in 'all parts' of the Chinese Empire. It would be easy to exaggerate the contemporary importance of these pronouncements. They were not accepted in good faith by the other powers, though Hay sought to promote the impression that they were. They were little more than gestures, in the immediate sense of the term. But they entered deeply into the American view of the Orient in the future; and they had too a moral influence that entitles them to an important place in the history of American foreign policy.

The Open Door notes express an interest in China that has been a powerful factor in the forming of American policy. From what was this interest derived? It is always hard to answer this type of question (which involves analysis of motive) with assurance. But there are two observations that may be made. On the economic side, Americans have long seen in China a vast and undeveloped market, and have assumed, probably over-optimistically, that here was one of their great chances for investment and trade in the future. On the moral side, American missionaries have been tremendously interested in China, and this interest has spread through them to thousands of small communities all through the United States. Their influence at the State Department has been very real; and this is by no means the only case in which factors other than self-interest have stirred the American mind and determined the choices of diplomacy. On the cold and cynical basis, the United States has, for a long time, had a greater financial stake in Japan than in China, and a greater commerce, and should have favored the first of these two nations and watched its career of imperialism with tolerance; but the facts, as we shall see, have been far otherwise.

There is another interesting episode connected with the activity of the McKinley administration in China. In 1900 there occurred an outburst of Chinese nationalism known as the Boxer movement. The foreign legations in Peking were besieged, and an international force had to be sent to relieve them. To this international force the United States contributed, a significant departure from the no-entanglement precepts of the Fathers. Association with other states came easier in the East, obviously, than in the West; and this fact was to be of some importance in breaking down the isolationist complex in the years ahead. In a limited sense (too much should not be made of the generalization) America was to enter Europe through the back door in some of the activities of its diplomacy.

The years of the administration of Theodore Roosevelt were to see significant changes in the Orient and witness the rise of Japan as a great power. They were also to see a sharp exchange in the relations of Japan with the United States. At the turn of the century the skies appeared serene. The Japanese as they sought to check the encroachments of Imperial Russia in Manchuria and in Korea, had, on the whole, the sympathy of most Americans. When war broke out in February 1904, public sentiment ranged itself chiefly with Nippon. And the good offices of the President, by which the controversy was ended, and his direct participation in the making of the peace treaty, might have been expected to consolidate the good feeling that had existed up to this time. But it was by no means so. The President intervened in the discussions to persuade the Japanese government to renounce its claims to an indemnity; in Japan his activities were roundly denounced as unfriendly; and the beginnings of a new tension in American-Japanese relations date from this very episode. For its own part, the Japanese government, no doubt, was not sorry to have a scapegoat; and in any case the national self-confidence had been raised by the victories of war to a point where a slight bumptiousness was almost sure to make itself manifest.

At the same time there was brought up a new issue that was bound to affect unfavorably American-Japanese understanding. In 1906 the school board of San Francisco attempted to segregate the Japanese in the public schools. The Japanese protested that such action was in violation of treaty rights. The Roosevelt administration found itself in a difficult situation, a situation made even more difficult by the American federal system, which conferred no power upon the government in Washington to interfere with local matters. The matter was finally settled by a statesman-like compromise. Behind the question of the school children lay, of course, the much broader issue of immigration, already settled with regard to China, but not as yet faced in regard to Japan. In exchange for a withdrawal of the offending local ordinance by the San Francisco School Board, Roosevelt secured a 'gentleman's agreement' with the government at Tokyo, by which the Japanese themselves agreed to control, virtually to suspend, the movement of their nationals into the United States. This was a wise solution of a delicate problem; but it could not conceal the fact that here was, from the Japanese point of view, a grievance and an affront to the pride of a powerful and growing nation.

The President, before he left office, made one more decision that concerned Japan. He decided (and in this he acted much in character) that the Nipponese needed to be made aware of the physical strength of the United States, and in the years of 1908-9 he sent the fleet around the world. A judgment on this enterprise is not easy, but much later Roosevelt was to declare that this was 'the most important service that I rendered to peace.'

We must not think of American policy in the Orient in the days of 'King Theodore' as fundamentally provocative or aggressive. On the contrary, it strongly smacked of what Europeans describe as *Realpolitik*. Roosevelt made no protest against Japanese domination of Korea; and in the Root-Takahira agreement of 30 November 1908, in exchange for Japanese recognition of the Open Door and a mutual guarantee of respect for the territorial possessions of each nation in the Far East, the United States subscribed to the policy of maintaining the *status quo* in the Pacific area, which seemed to the initiated to involve recognition of Japan's newly-won special privileges in Manchuria. The President sought to create a new equilibrium in this part of the world; but balances of power are always precarious, and his efforts were hardly destined to outlast his own administration.

Japan was on the march. In the years of the Taft administration, she was consolidating her position in Manchuria; and futile gestures, unaccompanied by any possibility of invoking physical power, were a poor counteragent to her policy. The First World War gave her a larger opportunity. She lost no time in seizing the German-held port of Tsingtao, in the Chinese province of Shantung. In the famous Twenty-one Demands, she sought still further privileges in China, indeed, what was virtually a protectorate, and, though the most obnoxious of these demands were finally not pressed, they offered interesting evidence of the scope of Japanese ambition. In 1918, she occupied Siberia in opposition to the newly-constituted Government of the Bolsheviks.

The United States was hardly likely to relish these various indications of expansion. But the circumstances were hardly propitious for effective opposition. At Paris, in the face of understandings between Japan and the European allies, Woodrow Wilson was obliged to recognize the transfer of German rights in Shantung to the Government at Tokyo in one of the bitterest surrenders that he ever made. In the case of Siberia, the United States reluctantly participated in the occupation of that vast province, and perhaps by so doing did something to draw the teeth of Japanese ambition. In the case of the Twenty-one Demands, the American administration filed a caveat in regard to the future in a notable dispatch of 11 May 1915 by Secretary Bryan, in which it was declared that it could not 'recognize any agreement or undertaking impairing the treaty rights of the United States and its citizens in China, the political and territorial integrity of the Republic of China, or the international policy commonly known as the open door policy.' It was, conceivably, wise to issue such a warning; but, practically speaking, the American admonition was nothing more than thundering in the index, and affected in no very striking way the course of events.

At the end of the First World War the position of Japan in the

Orient had undeniably been much strengthened. Her position in Manchuria was more solid than ever; she had possession of the former German base in the province of Shantung; she had annexed and brought under virtually complete control islands of strategic value in the far Pacific; her troops were still in Siberia. Yet there were some respects in which she was less strong than she appeared. The war had been a financial drain, and the Japanese business classes were anxious for a period of quiet and opposed to a policy of adventure. One principal source of strength, the alliance with England, first made in 1902 and frequently renewed, was in somewhat shaky condition. Too ambitious a policy would have meant the possibility of a challenge to the two great English-speaking peoples in the Far East. Such challenge would, in any case, have required great audacity; it was made less likely by the fresh memory of a war fought in common. Japanese diplomacy in the nineteen-twenties proved on the whole, therefore, to be cautious and circumspect.

As for the United States, it, too, desired a period of normality after the exertions of the war years. There was, as is likely to be the case after a war, immense pressure for economy. There was also a very real peace sentiment which, partially frustrated by the failure of the United States Senate to ratify the treaty of Versailles (see CHAPTER VI), was looking for some other means of expression. The circumstances were thus propitious, from many points of view, for an attempt at reconciliation of American and Japanese interests.

Besides the political questions that have already been touched upon, it is important to notice one other matter, the naval rivalry between the United States and Nippon. The American government had by 1916, under the stress of the war and the difficult situation in Europe, embarked upon an important naval program. This program was viewed with natural distrust at Tokyo and resulted in a Japanese program that was, very distinctly, an answer to it. American insistence upon a large navy could hardly appear otherwise than as a threat to Japan. The Germans had been annihilated; the British were friendly. What else, therefore, could American building mean than that a vigorous policy was intended in the Orient? How maneuver effectively to check such a policy? A direct challenge, in the existing circumstances, was extraordinarily risky; the methods must be the methods of diplomacy. Thus, despite the intensity of feeling that made understanding difficult, the fundamental factors pointed towards a peaceable solution of the rivalry of the two nations in 1921.

It was the United States that took the initiative (though the British were ready to suggest that it do so) in calling a conference to meet at Washington in November 1921. This conference was to discuss the whole problem of armaments; but, since politics and physical power go together, it was also to concern itself with the problems of the Far East. The other nations concerned accepted, the Japanese a bit reluctantly; and the conference convened at the appointed time. It got under way with a dramatic proposal made by Mr. Hughes, the American Secretary of State, in his opening speech, calling for a scaling down of naval armaments according to a prearranged and carefully calculated schedule, which would accord parity to Great Britain and the United States, and a ratio of 60 per cent to Japan and of 35 per cent to Italy and France, the two principal Continental naval powers.

Rarely has a stroke bolder than that of the Americans been undertaken. It called for drastic sacrifices on the part of the American government itself, but at the same time asked much, also, of others. It gave the United States parity with Great Britain (which, for some mysterious reason, had become a point of sentimental importance with large elements of American opinion), and it fixed Japan in a position of permanent inferiority. It applied, it is true, only to capital ships; but it was sure to furnish a precedent for more widespread limitation in the future. It was received in stunned silence by the diplomats and with transports of enthusiasm by the mass of American opinion. It was hailed as a sign of a new era in diplomacy.

But then the bargaining began. The Japanese retained their Oriental *sang-froid,* as was to be expected; and, before the arms limitation agreement was concluded, they had added to it an all-important and fundamental condition. They extracted from the United States a promise not to fortify Guam or the Philippines. In other words (and the statement is not too strong), they demanded that the United States abdicate its physical power in the Orient, that it adopt such policies as would make it impossible, except after war and long delay, to match the power of Nippon. This was an immense concession; but American opinion, by this time, would not have understood the failure of the conference, and the concession was made.

As a result of the understanding on naval matters, it was possible to arrive at what then appeared satisfactory solutions of many of the political problems of the Orient. In the famous Nine-Power Treaty, the principles of the Open Door were for the first time incorporated in a solemn international compact, which the Japanese pledged themselves to observe; a compromise solution was found for the vexing question of the Japanese occupation of Shantung; assurances were given (and followed up) for the Japanese evacuation of Siberia. Looking at the matter broadly, the men of Nippon gave large assurances of good behavior for the future; and, from the American point of view, the engagements of Washington could be justified on the most approved liberal grounds. It could be argued, it *was* argued at the time, that Japan, free from any physical threat from the United States, would pursue a moderate and reasonable policy in the Orient, and that the way had been paved for such a policy. A spirit of optimism with regard to the East seemed justified by the achievements of American statesmanship. Few accomplishments of American diplomacy have been more generally praised than the accomplishments of the conference of Washington.

Yet, to the careful analyst, the conference adumbrated a shift in political alignment that was to become very obvious in another two decades. For one of the results of the meeting was to alter the character of the Anglo-Japanese alliance, a cardinal element in the stability of the Far East in the past two decades. In the United States, there had been from an early period some apprehension that this alliance might be directed against America. As early as 1911, the British had sought to exorcise this fear by inserting in the alliance a provision that it should not be valid against any nation with which Britain had a treaty of general arbitration, and by then proceeding to negotiate such a treaty of general arbitration with the American government. But the Senate failed to ratify the arbitration compact, and this ingenious expedient failed. At the end of the First World War, there was still a feeling that something had to be done about the matter. When the British Dominions met in London for the Imperial Conference of 1921, the Canadians, who sympathized with the point of view of their great neighbor, insisted with great force and with success that the alliance should not be renewed.

The question for British diplomacy at Washington was to get rid of the treaty with the minimum offense to Japan; and British diplomacy, as so often, was equal to the course of judicious compromise. There was devised what came to be called the Four Power Treaty, to which France, Great Britain, Japan, and the United States were signatories. The contracting parties bound themselves to refer future disputes between them to a joint conference and to respect each other's rights in the area of the Pacific. They also, in a remarkable paragraph, which has no meaning at all unless it was directed against Russia, bound themselves, in case their rights were threatened by another power, to 'communicate with one another fully and frankly in order to arrive at an understanding as to the most efficient measures to be taken, jointly or separately, to meet the exigencies of the particular situation.' Thus the alliance, as a possible instrument of action against the Americans, was dissolved; and a vaguer and less binding type of association was devised, which might, at least in theory, cover the case of Slav aggression in the Orient. In this reshuffle the United States secured, for whatever it might be worth, a guarantee of the Philippines against attack.

But, more than was realized at the time, the abrogation of the Anglo-Japanese alliance was a turning point in the East. For the time being, Japan might pursue a conservative policy and seek no new associations to balance what she had lost; in course of time, however, she would do so. The Japanese shift to the Axis powers, though long delayed, was prepared for by the events we have just described.

VI THE UNITED STATES, WORLD WAR I, AND THE 'TWENTIES

THE war with Spain had enormous consequences that reached far beyond the boundaries of the New World. It dramatized the entrance of the United States on the stage of world politics; a nation so buoyant, so rich, so populous, so filled with self-confidence, could no longer be excluded from the calculations of European statesmen; and, perhaps more than most Americans realized, their government began to be courted by the chancelleries of the Old World.

The principal courtier was Great Britain. At the end of the century Britain was beginning to face a new rival in Europe in the German Reich. Its sea power was challenged for the first time in many, many years by the German naval legislation of 1898. Its diplomatic position, at the same time, was one of isolation. It was the task of British statesmanship, attempted and carried through with consummate skill in the first decade of the twentieth century, to find for itself friends and allies in the struggle that was already adumbrated. And in this task one essential element was friendship with the rising Republic across the seas.

In the course of the long period between the Peace of Ghent and the war with Spain, there had been many controversies between Britain and the United States. There still existed in many Americans a dislike of this most powerful nation based upon a receding, but still remembered, past; and the Irish emigration to the New World, and the ineptitude of British policy in relation to this engaging, if hardly tractable people, operated to reinforce a sentiment that was in any case widespread. But even so, not a single dispute between the two countries had resulted in war; on the whole, even in this period Britain had been almost invariably reluctant to challenge American opinion in the ultimate sense of the word; and it was not difficult for

British statesmen to guide their policy with a view to friendship with the United States.

In the war with Spain, which was almost universally regarded on the continent of Europe as a brash and unjustifiable exercise of national power, the British Foreign Office was careful to make clear its sympathy with the American administration; the negotiation of the Hay-Pauncefote Treaty, already mentioned, was a remarkable example of concession without any *quid pro quo* but the friendly sentiment it might arouse; when the blockade of Venezuela took place in 1902 and American opinion reacted unfavorably, the British were quick to pay obeisance to the Monroe Doctrine; and, in a dispute between Canada and the United States over the Alaskan boundary, the final settlement by arbitration was attained through the action of a British judge on the arbitral tribunal, who, no doubt, in espousing the American side of the case, was acting with the encouragement of Downing Street. There were better and worse moments in Anglo-American relations in the years 1900-1914; but, on the whole, the atmosphere was one of increasing cordiality; the general arbitration treaty of 1911 (even though it failed of ratification in the Senate) was an example of the trend of affairs, and the two peoples were preparing to celebrate a hundred years of peace when the World War broke out in 1914. British diplomacy in this period had certainly accomplished something important in predisposing the United States to its own side of the matter in the world conflict that was developing.

Let us say here and now that there was nothing immoral in this objective. To some Americans the British courtship has always seemed too clever and too self-interested to be admirable; but why should not Great Britain have sought American friendship? And why should that friendship not have been reciprocated in so far as it accorded with the national interest of the United States?

The Germans also sought to ingratiate themselves with the Americans in the years between 1898 and 1914. In 1902 Prince Henry, the Kaiser's brother, came to the United States on a mission of good will, and in the years following, the Emperor himself carried on a friendly correspondence with the ebullient President of the United States. But, somehow or other, the results were not very satisfactory. At Manila Bay, in the course of the war with Spain, a German squadron appeared, actually superior in force to that of Admiral Dewey, and there some friction resulted. The extent of the misunderstanding was much exaggerated; but the legend of German unfriendliness took root, and no doubt it had been encouraged by the fact that news of the incident came through the British cable at Hong Kong. At the time of the blockade of Venezuela, the German government was unable to express its cordial acceptance of the Monroe Doctrine because of its chauvinist elements at home; and here again there was to develop a legend, already under way by 1907, to the effect that President Roosevelt had prevented some sinister enterprise on the part of the Reich only by pronouncing a virtual ultimatum to the German ambassador in Washington. Moreover, with the Roosevelt period, a new interest in the Navy was developing, an interest which, in our present perspective, can only be applauded; but with it came, on the part of many American naval officers, a tendency to view Germany as a rival; and the partisans of the movement in general found it sometimes convenient to point to the new and aggressive power (as they were quick to describe it) that was developing across the seas. The Emperor, by his utterances, more than once set Germany in unfavorable contrast with Great Britain; for 'divine right' was, naturally, distinctly uncongenial to Americans, while to the more instructed the democratic character of the British regime became fairly clear. There was then a distinct predisposition toward one of the two sets of belligerents when war came in 1914.

In the years from 1898 to 1914, however, the United States made only hesitating steps toward a role in world politics. It sent its delegates to the two so-called peace conferences at the Hague; under President Roosevelt it took a hand in the controversy that arose in 1905 over Morocco, and for the first time participated in a European conference, the Conference of Algeciras, called to reconcile the conflicting views of France and Germany on the Moroccan question; but the Senate, in ratifying the resulting agreement, expressly asserted the policy of non-interference in European affairs; and under President Taft, in a period of gathering diplomatic crises, the State Department kept its hands off almost entirely, so far as the Old World was concerned. The United States, when the World War broke out in 1914, was inclined to neutrality by its long and deeply cherished tradition; any other course would have been impossible; and even Theodore Roosevelt, never wholly displeased by the possibility of war, associated himself with the policy of the Wilson administration.

But it needs to be stated categorically that neither the administration nor the American people was at any time after July 1914 neutral in thought or impartial in attitude, although they were officially exhorted to be. President Wilson, by his whole training and experience, was an admirer of British institutions, British poetry, British character; his excursions to Europe had never carried him to the Continent, save for a brief visit to Paris; and his naturally pacific temper reacted against the militarism of Germany. His Secretary of State, Mr. Bryan, took a different view; but Mr. Bryan was inexperienced in diplomacy, and in the Department men like Robert Lansing wielded a substantial influence in favor of Britain and her Allies. In addition the President's most intimate friend, Colonel Edward M. House, was distinctly prejudiced in favor of Britain; indeed, he had, two years before the outbreak of war, published a remarkable book in which the future peace of the world was based upon an Anglo-American alliance.

The American people were no less predisposed to the Allied side than were most of the key men in the administration. After all, to the untrained mind (whatever the researches of postwar historians might disclose), it was the Austrians and the Germans who had begun the war; the German invasion of Belgium was a flagrant breach of international law, and just such an act as would arouse the innate sympathies of Americans for a weak nation; and the exploitation of German ruthlessness in the American press, not always with entire accuracy, could not fail to produce its effect upon the American mind.

Subconsciously, too (and the matter deserves more study than it has received), there was a feeling that the victory of such a power as Germany might be dangerous to the future security of the United States; Wilson himself very early in the struggle spoke of the possibility of a militarized world if Germany won; and, though Wilson never stated such views in public, there were not a few other partisans of the Allies who did so.

It is not strange, therefore, that the administration witnessed the British violations of international law with considerable complacency, and gave to the protests it felt compelled to make a somewhat *pro forma* character. But the German declaration of submarine warfare in 1915 (in the German view, an act of retaliation against the illegal acts of Britain) produced quite a different reaction. It involved a breach with a long-standing practice by which merchant vessels were exempt from destruction unless provision had been made for the safety of their passengers and crew; it concerned the destruction of life, not, as in the case of British action, the mere seizure of property; and it shocked the conscience of 1915 in a way that is difficult for the present generation, accustomed to the ruthlessness of modern warfare, to comprehend. Moreover, the Germans themselves intensified American feeling by an act that was not premeditated, but was none the less shocking. The first American life lost as a result of the submarine was that of an American seaman on a British ship; and Mr. Bryan stoutly contended that in this case there was no justification for a vigorous protest and that those who traveled on belligerent vessels did so at their own risk. But, while the administration hesitated, a German submarine commander sank the great British liner *Lusitania,* with a loss of 128 American lives. An explosion of indignation followed in the United States; and, after this grisly episode, it would have been difficult for the administration to retreat in practice from the position that it had, from the outset of the undersea war, asserted somewhat equivocally in theory, that the destruction of American lives on vessels either neutral or belligerent was a violation of international law. From this moment forward it was almost certain that, if the Germans persisted in the use of the U-boat, they would bring the United States into the struggle.

In later days the thesis was to be put forward that other factors brought the United States into the war, that America finally intervened to protect the loans which it made to the Allies to safeguard its war prosperity, in obedience to the propaganda of the British. But the timetable of events shows that by May 1915, when the *Lusitania* was sunk, the war loans were as yet nonexistent, that American prosperity was only in the germ, that the British propaganda machine had hardly got into high gear. To lead a democratic people into war is no easy matter; it requires an issue that can be stated in generally acceptable terms; and the submarine warfare was such an issue. No careful historian would possibly assert with confidence that without the submarine issue the Americans would have gone to war; such a statement would be a gross example of history by hypothesis; while the statement that the rupture finally came on the submarine issue is too clear to admit of dispute.

President Wilson, however, with what his admirers have always contended was true statesmanship, first essayed to settle the issue by negotiation; he succeeded in extracting from the Germans first a pledge not to sink liners and then a complete renunciation of the

U-boat warfare. That the country appreciated these efforts for peace was proved when the President was re-elected by the votes of the South and West in 1916 in a campaign in which the Democratic rallying-cry was that he had 'kept us out of war.' His position was that, if the country was to enter the conflict, it must enter it united; and his note writing and negotiation found its justification in just this theory. In the meanwhile the country began to prepare itself; the President himself became a convert to that cause by the winter of 1916; and the nation, when it finally made its momentous decision, was at least more ready than it had been when the *Lusitania* went down. No doubt Britons and Frenchmen still find it hard to forgive the delay of the United States; but, viewed from the purely American standpoint, the reasons for this delay are comprehensible, and, in many people's views, compelling.

Once the United States had entered the war in April 1917, the President much altered the tone he had taken during the long period of neutrality. He now found the Germans to be a menace to the peace of the world and to the security of democratic nations; and, sublimating the issue—as a great statesman always seeks to do—he put before the American people the hope that the war might end in an international association of the nations for the maintenance of peace. This idea, first appearing in 1915 and owing much to the statesmanship of Sir Edward Grey, had, in fact, begun to be popular in the United States in 1916, and had been endorsed by the President as early as May of that year. It had even been commended in the Democratic platform on which Wilson stood; but it attained an increasing significance with the actual entry into the conflict. It brought American peace sentiment to the support of the war; and it gave currency to a great and influential aspiration, which still exists, and has played a significant part in the unfolding of events.

Wilson's war diplomacy was marked by a truly remarkable leadership. No voice was more compelling than his. He soon laid it down as a fundamental principle that German militarism must be overthrown; and in the famous speech of the Fourteen Points (8 January 1918) he was able to give to the war aims of the Allies (mixture of idealism and selfish ambition that they actually were, of course) a definition that satisfied and inspired liberal opinion. True, the speech of the Fourteen Points did not accomplish one of its main objectives, the keeping of Russia in the war. In that great country the Revolution of 1917, originally moderate in character, had culminated in the Bolshevik *coup* of November 1917; and in the course of the next few months the regime of Lenin and Trotsky, intent on drastic internal change, made peace with Germany, despite the declarations of President Wilson. But, whatever disillusionments were to come, at the time that it was pronounced the speech of the Fourteen Points received a very warm reception in the Western world and gave to the President in the last year of the war a remarkable pre-eminence.

When the tide of battle turned in the summer of 1918 and the panic-stricken German military leaders began to look for a way out, Wilson again became the spokesman of the Allies and demonstrated the strength and clarity of his own purpose. In a series of masterly exchanges with the German government, he forced the beaten enemy from one position to another, compelling the evacuation of Belgium, the abandonment of the submarine warfare, and the acceptance of the Fourteen Points. Whether he was wise also to force, as in some measure he did, the abdication of the Kaiser, instead of contenting himself with a constitutional monarchy in Germany on the British model, is a question that might be debated; it seems possible, in our later perspective, that such a monarchy might conceivably have offered a better barrier to Hitlerian demagogy than the weak republic of the 'twenties and early 'thirties; but he was at least consistent in purpose.

Later generations were to accuse the President of having let Germany in for a soft peace, but the accusation is unjust. The terms of the Armistice of 11 November 1918 were fixed by the military and naval leaders; they were such as were intended and, in fact, successfully designed to make a renewal of German resistance impossible; and while it may be true that the fact that German soil escaped invasion made the completeness of the victory less evident to the people of the Reich than was desirable, it cannot fairly be said that Germany was not thoroughly and decisively beaten. That she was so beaten is the clear judgment of objective history.

And then came the difficult task of making peace, of satisfying the interests, the ambitions, and the passions of the great coalition that had fought the war. To a statesman of Wilson's type, such a task involved also fundamental questions of principle; the faithful observance of the not always precise language of the Fourteen Points, the recognition of the principle of self-determination, which he had frequently proclaimed in the course of the war, the foundation of the League of Nations, of which he had so often spoken. With so much at stake, it is not strange that the President determined to assume personal leadership in the task ahead, to go to Paris and there contend for a settlement sufficiently reasonable and just to win the support of the people of the United States and be guaranteed by the new international organization. The decision has frequently been condemned as unwise; it operated to cut off the President from the tides of opinion at home; it made it necessary for him to engage in a distasteful process of bargaining and negotiation in which his prestige was seriously undermined; it weakened his reserves of physical strength. Yet one of the most careful students of the subject has contended with much cogency that the treaty signed at Paris was undoubtedly a better treaty because of Wilson's personal influence; and even those who condemn him must pay tribute to the spirit in which he labored, 'standing,' as Professor Becker once put it, '. . . for decency and a measure of faith in human nature in the midst or suspicion and low intrigue.'

It is not necessary here to make a judgment on the pact of Versailles. Like every such political document, it could not fail to be a work of compromise, or to reflect in many of its terms the national selfishness that invariably awakens in the victors; but the heart of the matter lay, not in its terms, but in the manner in which it was carried out in practice over the years, enforced by the collective power of the victors—or peaceably modified. The President was well aware of its imperfections; but he counted—more and more as the negotiations advanced—on the gradual processes of accommodation and adjustment to remove its imperfections, and on the machinery of the League to remedy its most glaring defects. The world needed peace and needed it badly; the starting point toward that goal had to be found in an admittedly imperfect document. Yet it is not possible to conceal the fact that the League built at Paris lacked the power, especially the physical power, to maintain the new order; it was no stronger than the unity of the great nations that had played the principal role in bringing it into being; indeed, the Covenant provided no clear design for the chastisement, by force of arms, if need be, of an aggressor nation. The territorial terms of the treaty in many instances were drawn with a view to the principle of self-determination; many of the new state boundaries were to be determined by plebiscite; but where Wilsonian principles might run in favor of Germany, as in the possible union of the Reich with German

Austria, or in the case of the Sudetenland, the German-speaking region within the limits of Czechoslovakia, they were not applied. On the economic side, the reparations clauses were so drafted as to give infinite trouble; and, finally, the exclusion of Russia from the settlement was a most unhappy augury for the future, even though no other course was possible, given the character of the Russian Government and the violent prejudices which it had aroused among influential sections of both French and British opinion.

There is, however, one additional observation with regard to the compact of Versailles that ought to be made; in view of the events through which the world was to pass in the years 1939-45, it is naïve to imagine that it was possible, at the end of the First World War, to forge an instrument that would satisfy at one and the same time the sense of justice of the victorious Allies and of the beaten Germans; and it is equally naïve to assume that the spirit of aggression, of which Germany was to give so striking an example within a quarter of a century, could have been exorcised by *any* terms within the power of statesmanship to frame. To blame the weaknesses of the peace treaty for the grisly events of later years is certainly to take a very partial, if not an absolutely incorrect, view; and to weight more heavily the errors of the statemen at Paris than the errors that permitted the rebirth of German armed power in the 'thirties is to do a great injustice to the efforts that were made by President Wilson to lay the foundations of an enduring world order.

Nor must we omit all mention of his positive achievements. The founding of the League was, at least, a step in the right direction; the French designs for the separation of the Rhineland from Germany (a flagrant violation of the principle of self-determination) were checked by his opposition and that of Lloyd George; the French demand for the Saar Valley, with its coal fields, was attenuated by the institution of an international regime there, which was to last for only fifteen years, when the Saar inhabitants were to vote on their future status; the mandatory system established a measure of international supervision over territories inhabited by peoples not yet ready for self-government, where these territories were wrested from the enemies of the Allies; the Polish settlement was revised by Wilson and Lloyd George in the final days of the treaty-making, with a view to giving some recognition to German protests. Wilson tried to live up to his principles; and he won more than one victory.

His real defeat was to come at home; and for it he was, in no small measure, himself to blame. Very unwisely, as events were to demonstrate, he appealed to the American people for a Democratic Congress in the congressional elections of 1918; his appeal failed; and partisan bitterness, which might well have existed in any case, was accentuated when the Republicans carried not only the House but the Senate. At Paris, in the drafting of the Covenant, he honestly tried to meet criticism and made some changes in the draft of that document to allay opposition at home; but he took a truculent tone toward the Republican opposition that could hardly fail to irritate. As for his party foes, they were not themselves disposed to be magnanimous; Senator Lodge, chairman of the Committee on Foreign Relations in the Senate, hated Wilson with a venomous hatred; and men like Hiram Johnson and William E. Borah, less personal in their attitude, saw in the Covenant a breach with the whole American past and a defiance of the maxims of George Washington. It became clear in the summer of 1919 that the treaty could not be ratified without reservations; but Wilson stoutly insisted that these reservations must be only interpretative, and that the treaty must not be modified. This attitude was natural in a negotiator, and there were precedents for it; but it failed to correspond with the facts. Nor did Wilson's attempt to appeal directly to the people succeed; he collapsed in the course of a tour of the country in the fall of 1919. When the treaty came up for a vote, with reservations attached, it was defeated by the votes of the Republican isolationists on the one hand and the Wilsonian Democrats on the other; and efforts to revive it were futile. Wilson himself, in a supreme act of folly, demanded that the issue be carried into the presidential campaign of 1920, the worst possible place for it to be settled in view of the passions, the evasions, and the confusion that usually characterize the great quadrennial assizes of the American nation. In that campaign, the Republican candidate, Warren Harding, managed to carry water effectively on both shoulders; his overwhelming victory was followed by the definite abandonment of the treaty, and by a separate treaty of peace with Germany.

The election of 1920 is not hard to understand in the broad perspective of American history. The American people had hardly been prepared for the world role that was thrust upon them by the war; the old points of view still had great vitality; there were various racial groups that were in a bad mood, the German-Americans because of what they deemed to be the harshness of the peace, the Irish because of the campaign of repression the British were carrying on in Ireland, the Italo-Americans because Wilson had opposed some of the Italian claims at the peace conference. There was also a natural reaction against war controls and presidential leadership; the country wanted 'normalcy' (to use the new President's phrase), and with Warren G. Harding it certainly got it.

Yet American foreign policy in the 'twenties was not like American foreign policy before the First World War. It was strongly influenced by the vision of world peace that Woodrow Wilson had done so much to conjure up; it sought in various ways to interest itself in the Europe whose shape and form its armies and its statesmen had done something to fashion. There was, for example, a movement for the reduction of armaments; there was an attempt to bring the United States to the support of the World Court set up under the aegis of the League; there was, as time went on, more and more intimate co-operation with the League itself. There was, too, helpful participation in some important practical problems, such as reparations. This question was in a thorough mess by 1923. Immense sums had been declared to be due from the Second Reich by May 1921; the Germans, either from sheer incapacity to do so, or from a lassitude and disgust induced by the severity of the terms, fell behind in making payments; and, despite the opposition of the British, in the winter of 1923 French troops occupied the Ruhr. There followed German passive resistance; the debauching of the German currency until the mark was rendered worthless; the complete breakdown of the German financial system. In these circumstances the United States helpfully intervened. The Secretary of State, Mr. Hughes, proposed that a scientific determination be made of Germany's capacity to pay; the suggestion was accepted and commissions were appointed under American chairmen; and a scheme was formulated which, from the name of the most prominent American concerned, became known as the Dawes Plan. Germany was helped to its feet by a loan, mostly floated in the United States; a regular schedule of payments was worked out (though without limit of time); machinery of international control was set up under American supervision with a view to protecting Germany's exchange. When the Dawes Plan seemed to need revision, the same procedure was followed; the Young Plan came into being in 1929; but this time the whole problem of reparations was soon altered by the coming of the Great Depression.

But while, in the ways just mentioned, America was not unwilling to recognize the realities of its world position, in other ways it was far from accepting its new responsibilities. We can see today that it would have been better if the attempts to pay vast sums over frontiers in connection with war indebtedness had been abandoned; but one of the principal obstacles to such a course of action was American insistence upon the payment of the ten billion dollars it had loaned to its European allies. True, the United States, in a series of agreements, did scale down these debts; in some instances the concessions made were substantial; but these concessions were not sufficient to prevent complete default in the first years of the 'thirties. Moreover, the American government neglected to conform to an elementary principle of economics, that a creditor nation must be willing to receive imports in payment of the interest on its loans; on the contrary, the Fordney-McCumber bill of 1922 represented a return to that extreme protectionism which had been reversed by the Democrats but which was typical of Republican administrations; and the Hawley-Smoot bill of 1930 was even worse than its predecessor. More important, the Harding-Coolidge period was one in which not the slightest commitment could be made to give strength to the League machinery for the punishment of aggression; the United States would not even signify its willingness to take no action against an economic blockade brought about under the auspices of the League. Whether a different attitude would have made it possible to create an effective machinery of sanctions, of punitive measures, may be doubtful; but no one can deny that the attitude of the American government discouraged even the attempt to fortify the new international organization. The steps that were taken for the preservation of peace through the treaties of Locarno were taken without reference to the United States.

It was, perhaps, characteristic of the American people at this period that they were moved to put their faith in the Kellogg Pact. This remarkable agreement, negotiated and signed in 1928, bound the nations that adhered to it not to resort to war as an instrument of policy, but to settle all disputes arising between them by peaceful means; it was a peculiarly American product; it was negotiated by Secretary Kellogg, with the blessing of Senator Borah, chairman of the Senate Committee on Foreign Relations and a leading isolationist a decade before; and it was ratified by an overwhelming vote. Almost all the nations of the world appended their signatures. It represented (and the fact must be stressed) the naïve faith of the American people in paper promises, in mere pledges to be virtuous; it was a signal example of the reluctance of the American mind to face the fact that physical power is an incident, a necessary if unpleasant incident, to the conduct of international affairs. As has been wittily and wisely stated, you can no more separate power and politics than you can separate sex and marriage; you can sublimate power, as you can sublimate sex; but you cannot exorcise it by a wave of the magician's wand. A mature nation must face this obvious, if not agreeable, fact; but the Americans were certainly not mature, so far as international politics are concerned, in the decade of the 'twenties.

Finally, in considering this period from 1900 to 1929, we must introduce considerations that, to the uninstructed, may appear extraneous from the point of view of foreign policy; we must say a word on the subject of the American economy. The 'twenties were a period of remarkable prosperity; they ended in the greatest depression, in the most destructive economic downturn, that the United States had ever endured. It is idle to speak of these facts as if they had no relevance to the international scene. The American people, to put it bluntly, let their economic order go haywire; they ignored completely the possibilities of control, the wild speculation in the stock market, the flood of foreign loans ill-secured and often ill-advised; the pyramiding of business enterprises; the growing maladjustment between agriculture and industry. The structure that they built collapsed. That collapse brought suffering in its wake all over the world; in the third decade of the twentieth century it was impossible to insulate the United States from the countries of Europe; and, as on the other side of the Atlantic, the shadows deepened, the sinister forces of nationalism gathered strength. Out of the Great Depression came the success of National Socialism and the rise of the psychopathic demagogue who was to guide the destinies of the Reich from 1933 to 1945; out of the Great Depression came the rebirth of Japanese militarism; out of the Great Depression came the lassitude and the concern with internal problems that made it possible for the democracies to stand by inertly while the forces of aggression gathered strength. And the implications of the Depression extended further. For the first time for the uninstructed (unless the uninstructed were Marxists) came the question concerning the vitality of the capitalist order, its capacity to solve its problems or, at any rate, to avert widespread collapse and increasing disorganization. The events of 1929 are not a part of domestic history alone; they are of the very essence of the momentous problems of the next two decades. But this aspect of the matter deserves a chapter to itself.

VII THE 'THIRTIES

IN ORDER to understand the diplomacy of the 'thirties, it is necessary first of all to look briefly at the European scene. The collapse which came to the United States in 1929 was followed by a similar collapse in Europe; and the distress of these years was followed by a great resurgence of nationalism in Germany. There a powerful demagogue arose in the person of Adolf Hitler, and this sinister man exploited the suffering of the time to rise to the supreme power in the Reich. The process was not immediate; indeed as late as 1932 it seemed possible that the movement of National Socialism which Hitler headed would fall short of supreme power. But in 1933 the Fuehrer, as he styled himself, became the Chancellor; he soon made a mock of constitutional forms; and by 1934 he had become the undisputed master of the German people. In the first years of his power the re-markable recovery of Germany veiled the monstrous nature of his authority, and the rearmament which activated the German economy was not yet seen as the prelude to the great struggle that was to come at the end of the decade. The German government withdrew from the League of Nations; in defiance of previous engagements, in 1936 it occupied the demilitarized territory on the left bank of the Rhine; it made waste paper of the clauses of the treaty of Versailles which limited German armament. But it was only toward the end of the decade that the clouds began to lower ominously; in 1938 Hitler an-nexed the republic of Austria; in the summer and the fall he turned the heat on Czechoslovakia; and war was only averted by the con-ference at Munich, which gave the Germans control of the province of the Sudetenland, hitherto in Czechoslovak hands. In the midst of these events the French and the British were inert; it was not until the winter of 1939 that, with the total suppression of the Czecho-slovak state by the Fuehrer, the tide of feeling changed, and resistance to German aggression became the policy of both governments.

In the meantime what was the attitude of the government of the United States? It is not easy to take an active interest in the affairs of others when one has a pain in one's stomach; and the Americans in the nineteen-thirties had a very large pain indeed. It did not help that in the Hoover administration the Hawley-Smoot tariff, the highest in our history, obstructed the channels of international trade; a severe shock to many Americans came with the abandonment of the gold standard by Great Britain in the fall of 1931; and the repudiation of the war debt agreements of the 'twenties by most of the European nations, except Finland, naturally produced a painful impression in the United States. All in all, in such circumstances it was easy for the Americans to assume an attitude of aloofness, and to adopt a point of view, by no means unfamiliar in its history, that the nations of Europe were a dangerous and subtle lot, who needed to be viewed with a good deal of circumspection.

This new mood, interestingly enough, found powerful reinforcement in a spate of revisionist literature with regard to American entry into the First World War. The first important work on this subject was C. Hartley Grattan's *Why We Fought*; the most influential—no doubt influential because it was written with a skill and charm that is often denied to professional historians—was Walter Millis's *The Road to War*; the most indignant, yet buttressed with all the apparatus of scholarship and with a name of distinction, was Borchard and Lage's *Neutrality*. It was discovered by the writers of the revisionist school that the United States had been taken for a ride, that its prejudices resulted in a one-sided neutrality and in involvement in war; and it was more than hinted that sinister economic and political forces, the munitions trade, the loans, the British propaganda, were responsible for the unhappy result. The same view was popularized in a Senate investigation on the arms traffic, conducted by Senator Nye of North Dakota, of whose intellectual qualifications for his task and of whose capacity to weigh evidence it is charitable not to speak. The revisionists, in the judgment of the author of this study, were wrong. But the result of their agitation was a remarkable series of statutes, the object of which was to make entry into a new war impossible by forbidding the doing of those things that, it was assumed, had carried us into the first. Thus, the traffic in arms was forbidden; loans to warring states were banned; the President was first authorized and then required to keep Americans off belligerent merchant vessels (no *Lusitania*, the reader will observe); thus the Old World states so injudicious as to go to war were to come and carry away in their own vessels, and pay on the nail for, such commodities as the President should designate. All this was very fine; it was widely applauded at the time; and it seems to have occurred to only a few Americans that what the Congress of the United States had done was to assure Adolf Hitler, already plotting the spoliation of Europe, that America would interpose no obstacles to his projects of aggression. In our present perspective, this was certainly no worse, and conceivably a good deal less blameworthy, than the conduct of Great Britain and France; but it is doubtful, none the less, whether many persons would care today to defend the neutrality legislation of 1935-37.

It cannot be said that in this period President Roosevelt offered much opposition to the predominant public mood, whatever may have been, and undoubtedly were, his secret reservations. Indeed it may be stated with some assurance that had he chosen to oppose the legislation on which we have just commented it would have been passed over his veto by an overwhelming vote. Perhaps it should be said in explanation of his attitude that the problems of domestic reform and reconstruction were large and pressing; as late as 1939 there were still 9,000,000 unemployed; and the mood of the business interests of the country was by no means an exuberant one. The instinct which led him toward acquiescence is intelligible.

So much for the diplomacy of the United States in connection with Europe; let us turn to observe the situation in the Orient. The central question in this area was the emergence of Nationalist China, and the rebirth of militarism in Japan. In the 'twenties the skies had been relatively serene; the progress of the new China under the leadership of Chiang Kai-shek seemed to augur well for the future, while the Japanese, if they did not observe this progress with complacency, took no militant and open steps to oppose it. Nor were they disposed to a bellicose attitude in the area of armaments; at London, in the naval conference of the winter of 1930, they put their signature to a treaty that extended the principles of the treaty of Washington to all naval vessels, though with a slight concession on the matter of ratios. But by 1931 the scene had changed; and to some extent this change must be attributed to the economic crisis which was by that time well-nigh world-wide. A movement of intense nationalism now developed in Japan, fed by the discontent of the military with the concessions made in the treaties of previous date. Under the Japanese Constitution the Ministers of War and the Navy reported only to the Emperor; they were jealous of their privileged position; and in their determination to maintain it they embarked Japan upon a course of action which was to have momentous consequences and lead straight to the attack on Pearl Harbor in 1941. The first aggressive act, an act undertaken without the sanction of the civil authority, was the occupation of Manchuria in the fall of 1931. Following an explosion on the Japanese-controlled South Manchurian railway, the whole province was overrun; the violation of previous engagements was obvious; and the resentment aroused in Washington was, from the beginning, extreme—all the more so since the action was, to a large degree, unanticipated.

What should be done in such circumstances? The answer was an attempt on the part of the administration to rally international opinion against Nippon and to invoke the support of the League of Nations. Of this body the United States was not a member, and it had steadfastly refused to make any commitments in regard to its course in case of League action against an aggressor. Now, however, an attempt was made to prod the League Council into action. That body attempted, in vain, to arrest the march of the Nipponese; failing in this, it appointed on 20 October an international commission of five members, which was to visit the Far East and report on the international situation there. It is possible that the American Secretary of State, if he had had his way, would have gone further; there was some talk of the invocation of economic sanctions against Japan.

Before the Lytton Commission, as it was called, had reported, Secretary Stimson took another important step. On 7 January 1932, in an identic note to China and Japan, he promulgated the doctrine that was to bear his name, and declared that the United States 'does not intend to recognize any situation, treaty, or agreement which may be brought about' by resort to war. Moreover, American diplomacy was successful, in the months that followed, in securing an endorsement of this new doctrine from the Assembly of the League of Nations.

The Stimson Declaration raised a question that is recurrent in diplomacy. Is it wise to assume a moral position when there is no intention of bringing physical power to bear? On the one hand, it may be argued that such action is necessary to the satisfaction of an aroused opinion in a democratic state, and that it makes up a record that may be useful to refer to in the future. On the other hand, it

seems to smack of futility and to irritate the nation against which
it is directed. To be 'willing to wound and yet afraid to strike' is, in
the view of many persons, very far from good diplomacy.

Certainly the phrase just quoted accurately describes the position
of the United States in 1932. Even an economic boycott against
Nippon, though discussed, was not favored by the administration.
And, in the long run, nothing very effective was done to check
Japan. True, the Japanese troops that landed at Shanghai in January
were, after a fierce struggle with the Chinese and eventual success,
withdrawn. But the Japanese went ahead and set up a puppet state
in Manchukuo; and when the Lytton report condemned their action,
though suggesting a very moderate compromise between Chinese and
Japanese interests, the government at Tokyo withdrew from the
League of Nations. It is hard to see in what respects the Stimson
diplomacy had succeeded; and in one sense it left a bitter taste in the
mouth, for it had revealed the futility of the League and the reluctance of European nations to take action against aggression. In particular, throughout the course of the events we have been describing,
the position of Great Britain was equivocal and unsatisfactory. The
Manchurian crisis weakened the structure of world peace immeas-
urably; it encouraged the Japanese to press forward.

The first year of the Roosevelt administration was a relatively quiet
one, so far as the Orient was concerned. It is at least possible that, if
the Japanese had been content to stop and digest their conquests, the
Manchurian controversy would have been allowed to fade out. Instead, however, under the leadership of the militarists, the government at Tokyo went on to assert extreme claims to a special position
in the Far East in the famous Amau declaration of the spring of
1934. At the end of the same year, moreover, it denounced the naval
treaties of Washington and London and launched upon a naval program that could hardly fail to be considered as a threat, and the details of which were carefully concealed from the public eye. Finally,
in July 1937, it began a war in China that looked to nothing less
than the overthrow of the Chinese Nationalist regime and the establishment of Japanese control over this vast and amorphous state.

The administration, even now, was not able to act effectively
against the Eastern imperialists. When Mr. Roosevelt, in October
1937, made a famous speech at Chicago in which he suggested that
law-breaking nations should be placed in quarantine, the response
from American public opinion was not such as to suggest that really

effective measures were at all likely. The conference called at the end of the year at Brussels, with eighteen nations attending, including the United States, could accomplish nothing but pious resolutions. Even the bombing of an American gunboat in the Yangtze, though the object of strong representations from Washington, was not viewed with much emotion by American public opinion. In a democratic state, it is public opinion which calls the tune; the administration, whatever its desires, could not have acted in the climate that then prevailed.

The mood of the American public in this period may be illustrated in another way; there arose a determined movement for a grant of independence to the Philippines. In this movement a number of factors were blended; the traditional American distaste for the direct government of others; the competition of Filipino products, especially sugar, with products produced in the United States, and the same generalized desire to reduce our international commitments which played a part in our policy toward Europe. Thus it was that by an act of 1934 the Filipinos were promised their independence by 1946, with a large grant of self-government in the intervening period.

We have said enough to illustrate the general disposition of the American people in the 'thirties to restrict the scope of their international action. If we contrast the diplomacy of the 'thirties with the far-reaching diplomacy of today, with commitments in every continent, it seems hardly credible that so extensive a lack of interest could ever have existed. Nor is it strange that those who enjoy historical speculation should ask whether many evils could not have been avoided if a positive note had been sounded by the State Department and the President in the period under review. But a more judicious assessment of the period would emphasize the fact that the disposition of the democratic nations to caution in this decade was a general phenomenon; and that a vigorous diplomacy is closely associated with economic health at home.

Nor is the span of years we have been examining entirely without positive interest, for the very factors which made the United States react against involvement abroad may well have given strength to the movement of Pan-Americanism, which is one of the most interesting features of the period, and one which has long-range importance superior to that of the policy in Asia and in Europe.

By the year 1928 there had already been foreshadowings of a pol-

icy of consideration and fair dealing to which, a few years later, was
to be given the name of 'good neighbor.'

Towards the end of the Coolidge administration, a change in the
American attitude towards the Latin American states became evident.
At the suggestion of Secretary Kellogg, Mr. J. Reuben Clark, an
officer of the Department, drew up a long analysis of the Monroe
Doctrine. Without explicitly renouncing the right of intervention,
Mr. Clark declared that such a right did not properly flow from the
declaration of Monroe. The memorandum which he prepared was not
published at the time, and indeed it never became the basis of declared
policy. President Hoover cautiously refused to permit it to be put
forward as the official position of the United States. But Secretary
Stimson appears to have sympathized with its point of view, and indeed stated so publicly. Moreover, the memorandum was published
in 1930, and was accessible to Latin American governments. It is of
significance, also, that in 1929, when the Senate was considering the
so-called Kellogg pact for the renunciation of war, Senator Borah submitted to the Foreign Relations Committee a gloss on the Doctrine,
which was appended to the instrument of ratification, and which, like
the Clark memorandum, dissociated interventionist principles from
the principles of 1823.

With such steps, however, the Latin American states could hardly
be satisfied. What they wanted was something more; what they
wanted was to see the rule of non-intervention written into an international convention. And this was what was attempted in the Pan-
American Conference of Montevideo, which met in the latter part of
1933. By this time, of course, the Roosevelt administration had come
into power. Mr. Roosevelt himself had, long before his inauguration,
in an article published in the important American magazine, *Foreign
Affairs*, in July 1928, expressed his discontent with the policy of
intervention (in which, incidentally, he had played a part a decade
and a half or so before) and had, in his inaugural, dedicated the United
States to what he there described as the policy of the 'good neighbor.'
His Secretary of State was also well-disposed toward concession to the
Latin American point of view. There were still, in the State Department, some reservations about going so far as to bind the United States
completely, and this sentiment was reflected in the final outcome of the
conference. The American government adhered to a protocol declaring
that no state had a right to intervene in the internal or external affairs

of another, but Mr. Hull made a declaration to the conference to the effect that by this agreement the United States did not waive its rights under international law.

The Senate of the United States, it is interesting to observe, ratified the protocol of Montevideo unanimously. The fact is important. For what it signalizes is the development of a nonpartisan foreign policy with regard to Latin America. Such a policy had up to this time been far from usual. Both parties, of course, had paid lip-service to the Monroe Doctrine. But the Democrats had criticized the Republican interventions in Nicaragua, and the Republicans had criticized the Democratic interventions in Haiti and the Dominican Republic; while in the same way neither the Mexican policy of Wilson nor that of Coolidge had commanded universal approval. That a line of action could be found in 1934 on which both parties were heartily agreed was a step forward of great significance.

Encouraged by this universal approval, the administration went further. A treaty for the withdrawal of the American marines from Haiti had been under negotiation in the Hoover administration. It was now completed, and by the end of 1934 there was not an American armed force on the soil of any one of the American republics. In the case of Cuba, too, the administration acted in generous fashion. When it came into office, it was confronted by a serious revolutionary overturn there, which had been caused by the grossly tyrannical regime of President Machado, Cuba's nearest approach to a Fascist chieftain. The administration, it is true, withheld its recognition from the radical regime of Grau San Martín and, in this way, attempted to exert political pressure, contrary to the spirit of the convention of Montevideo. But when the Grau San Martín Government was succeeded by the more conservative administration of Colonel Mendieta, the United States not only recognized the new administration but negotiated a treaty that abrogated the Platt amendment and removed the limitations of Cuban sovereignty that had been imposed in 1902. Here, again, it had the cordial support of the Senate of the United States. At the same time, there took place an important piece of economic statesmanship. Cuba, as a great sugar-producing state, was to a high degree interested in the American market. Its place in this market had been cut down by the Hawley-Smoot Law. But now the Jones-Costigan Act, establishing quotas for sugar imports, gave the island republic a chance to dispose of at least a substantial part of its sugar in the United States, and reduc-

tions in tariff duties redounded also to the interest of the sugar-grow-
ers. By these arrangements, it was made clear that the policy of the
good neighbor had wider implications than those contained in purely
political understandings.

What was begun in 1933 and 1934 was destined to be continued
on an increasing scale and in circumstances that gave high importance to the good-neighbor policy. The clouds were beginning to
lower in Europe; and, as the skies darkened, President Roosevelt,
with the political prescience that so often distinguished him, began
to move toward such a common understanding between the states
of the New World as would be of mutual value when war in Europe came. At his suggestion, the Argentine government called a
specific conference, to be concerned with the preservation of peace,
to meet at Buenos Aires in December 1936; and at this conference
the United States put forward a proposal for mutual consultation in
case of any threat from the other side of the Atlantic. The Argen-
tines, it is true, were not much interested. Their foreign minister,
Saavedra Lamas, had an antiwar treaty of his own, to which he attached an importance almost as great as was his personal vanity. But
Secretary Hull managed to deal with this exceedingly touchy man
with much skill; and a convention was signed along the lines of the
American plan. True, it lacked machinery for its practical execution;
but it represented a step forward, at any rate, along the lines of common action.

By 1938, at Lima, it was possible to go still further. There the
convention of Buenos Aires was implemented by an agreement that,
in case of possible aggression from abroad, the ministers of the American states would meet in the various capitals in turn, at the request
of any one of them. This understanding was no doubt made possible
by the near approach to war in Europe connected with the Czechoslovak question, which was only avoided by the capitulation of the
Western powers at Munich. The great coalition of the American
states was one step nearer completion. Thus the way was paved for
that successful co-operation with the states of the New World which
signalized the troubled years between 1939 and 1945. To these years
we shall soon turn.

There is, however, one final observation on the decade which
ought to be made. In no other period of our modern diplomatic history is the influence of the Congress over the Executive more ap-
parent. The whole tone of the neutrality legislation was set by the

national legislature, whether wisely or not the reader may judge. The attitude taken toward the Orient, and especially the law providing for the independence of the Philippines had a legislative origin. The policy of the 'good neighbor,' though due in a preponderant degree to the action of the Executive, was, as the unanimous ratification of the protocols of Montevideo and Buenos Aires proves, in perfect accord with the Congressional mood. The fact is one to remember. The President is often thought of as the director of American foreign relations, and such, in fact, he is. His power should not be underestimated. But he possesses no such freedom of action as the Prime Minister of Great Britain, or the Chancellor of Germany, to cite only two examples. On the composition of the national legislature the success of our foreign policy inevitably depends, in no small degree.

VIII   THE COMING OF THE WAR

IN THE preceding chapter we have indicated that President Roosevelt gave few signs of alarm at the danger from German and Japanese militarism during the greater part of the 'thirties. In 1936 at the Pan-American conference of Buenos Aires, as we have seen, he did indeed promote an agreement for mutual consultation in the event of aggression from the Old World, and this agreement was strengthened at the conference of Lima. But his attempt to rouse public opinion against Nippon in 1937 fell flat; and the moral homilies which Secretary Hull directed to Tokyo were hardly calculated either to rouse the American people or deter the aggressors. It is fair to say that in this period the navy was being built up, but the first strenuous note of warning came with the President's message to Congress in the beginning of 1939.

There comes a time in the affairs of men when they must prepare to defend not their homes alone, but the tenets of faith and humanity on which their churches, their governments and their very civilization are founded. . . . We know what might happen to us if the new philosophy of force were to encompass the other continents and invade our own. We, no more than other nations, can afford to be surrounded by the enemies of our faith and our humanity. The world has grown so small and weapons of attack so swift that no nation can be safe in its will to peace so long as any other single powerful nation refuses to settle its grievances at the council table. . . . In our foreign relations we have learned from the past what not to do. From new wars we have learned what we must do. We have learned that effective timing of defense and the distant points from which attacks may be launched are completely different from what they were twenty years ago. We have learned that long before any overt military act aggression begins with preliminaries of propaganda, subsidized penetration, the loosening of ties of good will, the stirring of prejudice and the incitement to disunion.

These words of warning were followed by an attempt to modify the legislation of the previous period; the President now called for the repeal of that portion of the previous enactments which forbade the export of arms and materials of war to *all* belligerents, thus placing the attacker and the attacked on a similar footing. For a time Congress could not be stirred to action; but in September momentous events occurred. We have already referred to the suppression of the Czechoslovak state in the spring; this event produced a revolution in French and British policy; and belatedly, but as the event was to prove, resolutely, both the French and the British governments entered into an alliance with Poland, the probable object of Hitler's next aggression. The aggression came; by a shameless bargain with the Soviet Union the German leader protected himself from the East, and agreed to the partition of the Polish state, and on 2 September 1939 the German armies crossed the Polish frontier, inaugurating a war that was to last more than five years, and to involve the greater part of the world.

To these events the President responded; convinced that the victory of Germany would be a menace to peace, he called Congress in special session and demanded repeal of the arms embargo, which had been denied to him earlier in the year, and by a vote that was strongly partisan in character, the Congress acceded. Even this step, however, was made possible only by accepting new provisions of the neutrality law, which authorized and directed the President to establish war zones from which American commercial vessels should be excluded.

Thus matters stood throughout the winter and early spring of 1940. It was a measure of American naïveté that many persons began to talk of a 'phony war,' as if Hitler were engaged in a kind of amiable pretense of aggression, rather than the real thing. Such illusions disappeared with the German occupation of Norway in April, with the invasion of Holland and Belgium in May, and with the collapse of French resistance in early June. The success of German arms, almost without a precedent in the history of Europe in its rapidity and scope, underlined the true nature of the Nationalist Socialist regime, and a thrill of terror went through many minds at what the future might hold. The President was equal to the occasion. In a speech at Charlottesville, Virginia, not far from the tomb of Jefferson, he pledged all-out aid to the defenders of democracy, and the speeding up of the national defense; and his action is the more creditable since it came in a year when he was a candidate for re-election, and under circumstances in which political courage is by no means always so forthrightly demonstrated. There is little question that he had caught the mood of the country; striking evidence of this fact was to be afforded when the Republican national nominating convention, meeting in Philadelphia, put aside the aspirants for the presidency who were isolationist or equivocal in their attitude, and nominated Wendell Willkie, an avowed supporter of assistance to the democracies. And additional evidence of the trend of public opinion is found in the passage by the Congress in the summer of 1940 of the first conscription act ever passed in time of peace, an act which bore the name of a Republican representative from New York and an anti-New Deal Democratic Senator from the Midwest.

The presidential campaign of 1940, therefore, did not turn on questions of foreign policy. As we have seen, the partisan spirit has often been evident in the conduct of foreign affairs. But, in this critical period for the United States, the dominant sentiment of the country was expressed by both candidates—with the customary electoral equivocations. Fortunately for the future, there was no sharp issue made up between those who wished to give assistance to the democracies and those who did not.

In the course of the electoral conflict the President ventured upon a bold and dramatic stroke. Invoking the full measure of his constitutional authority, perhaps more than the full measure, and obligingly sustained in his purpose by Attorney General Jackson, he negotiated an agreement with Great Britain in which fifty over-age destroyers were given to that hard-pressed nation, and in which the United States received in return the right to construct naval and air bases on the soil of various British colonies, stretching all the way from Cape Breton to Trinidad. Such a measure could be represented as defensive in character, as a thrusting of the American defense line eastward into the Atlantic; but it was also a signal service to the government in London, harassed as it was by the German U-boat warfare. And it met with widespread approval.

For the rest, it was necessary to wait until the campaign was over. But, once the President had been re-elected, he wasted very little time in bringing forward a plan for large-scale assistance to the enemies of Germany through what came to be called lend-lease. The bill for the authorization of this program, dramatically named H.R. 1776, was debated and acted upon in the winter of 1941. It was passed only after full deliberation; it was not signed until 12 March 1941; but it voted no less than seven billion dollars for the implementation of the new policy; and it gave the official sanction of Congress to a policy that could no longer, by any stretch of the imagination, be described as neutrality or by any less equivocal term than a quasi-alliance with Great Britain. There was, it is true, some partisan opposition to the measure; most of the votes cast against it were Republican; but it passed the House by a vote of 317 to 171, and the Senate by the still more decisive majority of 60 to 31. Its implications were not always recognized by those who supported it; it was often represented as a means of keeping out of war (which it was hardly likely to be); it represented a fundamental choice in the field of policy; and coming, as it did, only eighteen months after the outbreak of war, it stands in striking contrast to the careful efforts of Woodrow Wilson to maintain a neutral attitude a quarter of a century before.

The Lend-Lease Act, whether all those who voted for it recognized the fact or not, carried with it an inevitable corollary, namely, that the United States should see to it that the goods it was to send across the seas actually reached those for whom they were intended. Convoy, in the literal sense, was made difficult by the hue and cry of the isolationist groups, not yet reconciled to the policy of aid to Britain; but the President found a substitute for convoy in what were described as patrols, by which the American navy scoured the western Atlantic for submarines, reporting their position to the British. Moreover, in April an advance base for air patrol was secured by an agreement with the Danish minister in Washington for the occupation of Greenland; and this action, entirely unauthorized by the captive Danish government at Copenhagen, was justified in the name of the Monroe Doctrine. In July, a further step was taken when American troops replaced the British in Iceland, automatically extending the range of American action; and the close association of the British and Americans was still further dramatized when President Roosevelt and Prime Minister Churchill met in the waters of the western Atlantic and drew up the famous document known as the Atlantic Charter.

The Atlantic Charter was to the War of 1939-45 what the speech of the Fourteen Points and Woodrow Wilson's war address of 6 April 1917 were to the War of 1914-18: that is, an attempt to sublimate the issues, to dress in ideal language, language by no means insincere, the interests and objectives of the great English-speaking peoples. It enunciated certain general principles upon which the two statesmen rested their hopes for a better future for the world; declared against aggrandizement or territorial changes contrary to the will of the peoples concerned; supported the right of all peoples to determine the government under which they wished to live, and a fair and equitable distribution of essential produce between the nations of the world; and championed the idea of international economic and political collaboration for the maintenance of peace and the reduction of armaments, the raising of the living standards of the peoples of the world. At a later date, when the United States entered the war, its allies were, without exception, to subscribe to this far-reaching document. The Charter represents the recurrent tendency by which the leaders of democratic peoples elevate the minds and stouten the hearts of those whom they are called upon to direct in the harshest of all crises. It illustrates a fact that ought never to be forgotten: that the peoples of the United States and Great Britain, though like all peoples moved by a sense of national interest, desire in the great moments of their national action to mingle the idealistic and the practical in their formation of policy. Whoever does not understand this fact and whoever denies that it has important, and sometimes beneficent, practical consequences does not truly understand the foreign policy of either nation, and especially does not understand that of America.

While these great events were being enacted, on the stage of the world something else fully as portentous was taking place. On 22 June 1941, in what was to prove a decisive act of folly, Adolf Hitler launched the German legions against the forces of the U.S.S.R What would be the attitude of the United States toward this world-shaking step? What would be the reaction of the world's greatest capitalist nation toward an attack upon the land of Communism?

Before this question is answered, it is worth while to look at Russo-American relations in retrospect. They had been, officially speaking, nonexistent in the nineteen-twenties and early 'thirties. Republican administrations found in the Bolshevik regime a government so odious that they would not even recognize its existence, and they could justify their position by the Soviet repudiation of previous financial engagements and by the propaganda set in motion from Moscow. The Roosevelt administration, however, when it came into power, set a different course; perhaps it hoped for Russian assistance against Japan in the Far East; at any rate, whatever its motives, after an exchange of views with Mr. Litvinov, the Foreign Minister, it officially acknowledged the government at Moscow. The Great Depression, by accentuating the deficiencies of American capitalism, perhaps had made easier the acceptance of this Communist outsider. But it cannot be said that recognition produced cordiality; after a brief period of relative warmth, Russo-American relations grew chillier as the 'thirties advanced. They were naturally not helped by the cynical bargain made by the Soviets with Adolf Hitler in the summer of 1939 with regard to Poland. They were not advanced, either, by the Russian occupation of the Baltic states, whose independence had, from their very birth in 1919, been recognized by the United States; and they still further deteriorated after the Russian attack upon Finland, which seemed to many Americans to be such an act of bullying violence as could not possibly be defended. With such a background, it is not strange that American isolationists found in the German attack upon the U.S.S.R. an additional reason for a policy of abstention from intervention. Why not let the two Titans destroy each other?

But the risks of such a policy were immense, and they might have left Hitler with a vaster and more powerful empire than ever. The administration did not hesitate for a moment. It availed itself at once of the facilities afforded by the lend-lease enactment, and substantial quantities of munitions and implements of war began to move to the support of the hard-pressed Russian armies. No one can say precisely how decisive this support was; but it seems fair to assign it at least some weight in enabling the forces of Marshal Stalin to check the invader.

At the same time, the country moved nearer to entry into the European war. In September, taking advantage of a German attack upon an American vessel that was following the U-boat and reporting its position, the President went on the air and declared that henceforth United States patrols would sink Nazi 'pirates' on sight. He followed this step by asking of Congress the right to arm American merchant vessels and to lift the ban on American vessels' entering proscribed war zones. No doubt influenced in part by the sinking of two American destroyers, the national legislature responded to the President's appeal. But it did so with reluctance. The 'isolationists' made a last-ditch fight, and the legislation suggested by Mr. Roosevelt passed the House by the narrow vote of 212 to 194. No roll call could illustrate more eloquently than this, partisan though it may have been in large measure (137 Republicans voted in the negative), the deep-seated aversion of the American people to the decision that was being forced upon them.

Indeed, it might have been impossible for the United States to enter fully into the war had it not been for the events that occurred in the Far East. As the Japanese continued their career of conquest in that part of the world, there were indications of concern on the part of American opinion; in the summer of 1939 Senator Vandenberg introduced a resolution calling for the denunciation of the commercial treaty with Nippon. The State Department, anticipating its passage, acted on its own account; but for a time no further action of major importance followed.

Japan, in fact, while waiting to see what was the drift of affairs in Europe, had an interest in maintaining sufficiently good relations with the United States to permit the purchase of oil and aviation gasoline and steel scrap in the American market. Nor was the administration in Washington disposed to provocative measures. It wished to keep its hands free because of the peril from Hitler; it feared to take drastic action lest the Nipponese attack the defenseless Dutch East Indies. It had by this time begun an ambitious program of armament; the naval appropriation bills of 1938 and 1939 were of staggering proportions; but there was no intention of forcing the issue in the Orient.

But Hitler's dramatic victory in the spring of 1940, and the collapse of France altered the whole situation. In anticipation of trouble, the administration in July banned the export of oil and scrap metal without license, and followed this up with the restriction of aviation gasoline to the Western Hemisphere. The Japanese riposted without delay; in September they extorted bases from the French in northern Indo-China; and on the 27th of that month they entered into a formal alliance with the Axis, by which they bound themselves to attack any power that made war on any one of the signatories, and by which they secured a similar pledge in return. Here was a direct and shameless attempt to intimidate the United States and to confine its diplomatic action; the wonder is that it did not produce more resentment in the American press than was actually the case.

Yet it is probably true that Japan, though now leagued with Hitler, would have abandoned her new ally with the same cynicism with which she had adopted him, if only the price were right. The price—

and here is the crux of the matter—was our acquiescence in Japanese domination of China; and, we may be sure, it was a price which no American administration could have afforded to pay. Whatever the faults of the Chinese, whatever their inability to manage their own affairs with prudence or wisdom (and the judgment in these matters must needs be a harsh one), China had become by this time a symbol of principle; and the friendly sentiment the American people had always cherished for that great nation would have stood in the way of any diplomatic bargain. In the long diplomatic discussions of 1941 between Mr. Nomura, the Japanese ambassador at Washington, on the one hand, and Mr. Hull, the Secretary of State, on the other, there was much maneuvering for position, but never any agreement on the essential point. Nor was the diplomatic situation such as to make the Japanese more conciliatory as time went on. On the contrary, in April 1941, Mr. Matsuoka, the Japanese foreign minister, visited Moscow and signed a treaty of neutrality with the Government of the Soviet Union. He thus protected his country from an attack from the rear; while the Kremlin, fearing an assault from Germany, was glad enough to divert Japanese attention toward the basin of the Pacific.

The clouds in the Far East grew darker with the summer of 1941. The Japanese occupied southern Indo-China in July; the United States retaliated by freezing all Japanese assets and by cutting off trade. Such a measure had been frequently recommended by some of our diplomatic theorists as a sure means of bringing effective pressure upon the government at Tokyo; it had, as economic retaliation has often had, precisely the opposite result; it infuriated the Japanese and tended to make war more certain. True, the negotiations between Hull and Nomura continued, and in the fall of 1941 a special envoy, Saburo Kurusu, came to supplement the activities of the ambassador. On 20 November, the Japanese (and who could have honored their assurances?) declared that they would withdraw from southern Indo-China, evacuate the whole country upon the conclusion of peace, and agree not to make any armed advances in the South Pacific or in Southeastern Asia if the United States would co-operate in securing goods for Japan from the Dutch East Indies, restore commercial relations, supply Japan with required quantities of gasoline, and refrain from 'such measures and actions as will be prejudicial to the endeavors for the restoration of general peace be-

tween Japan and China.' In other words, if the American government would permit Tokyo to digest China at will, the Japanese
would temporarily limit their career of plunder. They would, they
suggested, even wriggle out of their engagements with Germany.
Thus was the treaty of 27 September 1940 revealed as a mere instrument of unqualified blackmail.

To the mind of an Oriental it may be that these terms seemed
such as might be accepted. The alternative, for the United States,
might be a war on two widely separate fronts, involving a national
effort the like of which had never been seen before, and risks com-
mensurate with those efforts; imperialism in the East was an old
story; why not let the Japanese engage in the usual game? Might not
China be better organized under the rule of Tokyo than it had ever
been under Chiang Kai-shek? But such considerations could have
no weight in Washington. Whether one likes it or not, the diplomacy of a democratic people, and especially of such a people as the
Americans, can make no such nefarious surrenders; the moral em-
phases enter into the diplomatic decision; indeed, time and again
they are controlling. Mr. Hull's response to the proposals of 20 November could hardly have been meant to be accepted; he called for
the evacuation of China, the recognition of Chiang Kai-shek, the
signing of a multilateral nonaggression pact. In exchange for these
very large concessions, he was willing to unfreeze Japanese assets in
the United States, to enter into a favorable trade treaty, to co-operate
in the stabilization of the yen.

Before this note was sent (which could hardly have resulted otherwise than in the termination or breakdown of the negotiations), the
voice of compromise had for a moment made itself heard. There were
some persons at Washington, especially in the armed services, who
were anxious to delay the challenge; a kind of *modus vivendi* was
proposed to tide over the tension; but the Chinese reacted so violently to this that the idea was dropped. Before this decision was
made, the Japanese carriers and submarines were on their way to the
notorious sneak-attack at Pearl Harbor.

Of that attack it is necessary to say little. It was a blunder as well
as a crime. It unified American opinion; it left no doubt whatsoever
about who was the aggressor; and it resulted in the only virtually
unanimous declaration of war in the history of the United States.
The militarists had committed the error characteristic of militarism;

they had ignored the difficulties that always stand in the way of final action by a democratic people when it comes to war, and had precipitated American opinion. In stupidity and recklessness, they had outdone their German rivals.

IX   THE DIPLOMACY OF THE WAR

With Britain, in the years from 1941 to 1945, there was maintained an alliance of unusual intimacy. The armed services of the two countries co-operated to a remarkable degree; and it was, as all the world knows, an American general who led the great and successful invasion of France in 1944 by the forces of the United States and Great Britain. The strategic conceptions of the two belligerents did not, it is true, precisely coincide; but the differences between them were never allowed to produce any real rift, and it may even be argued that the debate that took place on such issues actually redounded to the advantage of both. Politically, both powers early declared in favor of a policy of unconditional surrender; both favored the creation of an international organization for the preservation of peace at the end of the war; both wished to see a Europe reconstituted on the basis of self-determination and democratic government. Here again there was not undiluted accord; the British Prime Minister had little interest in the war in China; President Roosevelt, on his part, needled Mr. Churchill with regard to the grant of independence to India. In Italy, which fell to the Allies in 1943, the British were more favorable to the preservation of monarchical institutions than the Americans; in France, Britain found General de Gaulle, the leader of the Free French, perhaps no less difficult but more acceptable than did the government at Washington. But none of these differences profondly affected the course of the struggle, or postponed the hour of ultimate victory.

The real question of course was American relations with Russia. Despite the lavish aid given by the United States to the Soviet Union, aid which was fully justified as a necessary contribution to victory and which Stalin himself in an unguarded moment described as a major element in the struggle, the Russians never fully trusted the Americans, and only reluctantly made acknowledgment to their own people of the part played by the United States. We can see now that this was inevitable. The American dream and the Russian dream of the postwar world were bound to be different; Americans looked to a Europe reconstituted on a democratic basis, and committed to the gradual improvement of society within the existing fabric; the Communists, almost inevitably, looked to a world revolutionized and devoted to the teachings of Marx and Lenin. Since Russia was shut off to a substantial degree from the outside world, dominated by a leader who had never left Russian soil, and to whom intrigue and violence were natural, it is not strange that genuine cordiality never came to exist between Washington and Moscow.

No doubt the best moment in the alliance was at the conference of Teheran, late in 1943. There the leaders of the three great powers, Stalin, Churchill, and Roosevelt, agreed upon the general plan of military operations that was to follow; and the triumphant advance of both the Russian and Western forces from June 1944 till the final German collapse in May 1945 was evidence of what could be done by common effort. But before the war reached its end division began to appear; and the symbol of that division is to be found in the conference of Yalta, held in the winter of 1945.

By this time it was clear that Eastern Europe would come under the effective control of the Russian armies. The forces of the Soviet Union took Warsaw in the summer of 1944; they had advanced beyond the boundaries of prewar Poland into Germany by the winter of 1945. In such circumstances it is not strange that Stalin had determined to get his way in the areas which he controlled; and a large part of the debate at Yalta as to European affairs took place with regard to Poland. There was, of course, no open break; but the signs of the disruption of the alliance were clear. The Western powers had recognized and dealt with a Polish government-in-exile in London; the Russians, as they had advanced westward, had constituted at Lublin a new Polish regime, whose reddish color was perfectly obvious. The London Poles made their case more difficult by obstinate opposition to the drawing of Poland's postwar frontiers; they objected to the retention by the Soviet Union of the territories taken in the invasion of 1939. In the face of these facts the best that Churchill and Roosevelt could do was to sign an agreement with the Russians by which the Lublin regime was to be 're-organized on a broader democratic basis.' Future events were to demonstrate how illusory this promise was.

Already, too, at Yalta, was evident the essential difference of outlook between the West and the Kremlin with regard to the future of Germany, particularly illustrated in the question of reparations. The Russians, to put it bluntly, were bent on plunder; the West, especially Churchill, but also Roosevelt, drew back from policies that would impose on the democracies the economic restoration of Germany as a power of some consequence.

Nor were the events following the conference particularly happy. Though Stalin put his name to a Declaration of Liberated Europe which pledged the Allies to co-operate in the formation of democratic governments, committed to 'the earliest possible establishment through free elections of governments responsive to the will of the people,' within a matter of weeks, Mr. Vishinsky, the Deputy Foreign Minister, appeared in Bucharest, the capital of Rumania, and forced upon King Michael a government which was proto-Communist in character.

In April, Stalin accused, quite unjustly, the Western governments of coming to an agreement with the Italians which would 'permit the Anglo-American troops to advance to the East' and by which 'the Anglo-Americans have promised in return to ease for the Germans the peace-terms.' He even went so far as to say that as a result of this agreement the Germans on the Western front had stopped fighting. To these 'vile insinuations' Roosevelt responded with a firm denial; but the episode illustrated in vivid terms the Russian distrust of the West.

If this distrust was to a substantial degree damped down for a time, it was because of the situation in the Orient. The war with Japan was not yet ended; and it was the strong opinion of the American military authorities that it could not be brought to a final victory without the assistance of the Russians. This fact accounts for the negotiations on the future of China which took place at Yalta, and which were to be the subject of so many recriminations in the period that followed.

Before we examine these negotiations, it is necessary to say a word or two about the course of the war in the Far East prior to 1945. On the sea, and in the islands of the Pacific, the Americans, after the initial defeats, advanced toward victory; but the support received from their Chinese ally was hardly of a character to elicit enthusiasm. The plain truth of the matter is that the government of General Chiang Kai-shek was not a really strong government; it struggled constantly against a mounting inflation, which had a disastrous effect upon the national morale; but what was more important, it stood in great fear of the Chinese Communists, and was reluctant to commit its forces fully in the war against Japan with a resolute and dangerous enemy on its own soil. Long before the outbreak of the Great War, Mao Tse-tung and his supporters had established themselves in the province of Yenan; even before 1945 they constituted a growing force; and perhaps the Generalissimo is to be understood if he viewed them with suspicion and misgiving. The United States, on its part, could hardly regard China as the basis of its war policy in the Far East; it was naturally more concerned with the advance in Southeast Asia, and across the Pacific; and from the Chinese point of view, it gave scant support to the Nationalist government at Chungking. Its diplomatic efforts were also less than completely effectual; it sought to bolster Chinese prestige by the surrender of the rights of extra-territorial jurisdiction which it possessed in China; and at a conference in Cairo in 1943 it promised to Chiang at the end of the war the return of Formosa and the Pescadores, which Japan had filched from China in 1895, as well as the restoration of the Chinese position in Manchuria. But in 1944 the military situation in China was bleak; the Japanese had overrun the airfields from which, it was hoped, Chinese planes could bomb Japan, and it is not surprising therefore that Chiang Kai-shek played a minor role in American plans for ultimate victory.

On the question of Russian aid in the final phase of the war, there existed in 1945 a difference of opinion; the naval authorities, in view of the virtual destruction of the Japanese navy in 1944, in view of the crushing blows inflicted on the Japanese merchant marine, and in view of the increasing possibility of bombing raids on Tokyo, were disposed to think that Nippon could be brought to terms without invasion; but such was not the view of the military. To General Marshall, the Chief of Staff, and to General Douglas MacArthur, the commander in the Far East, Russian aid seemed vital.

As early as the fall of 1943, Marshal Stalin had assured Secretary of State Cordell Hull, on the occasion of Hull's visit to Moscow, that the Soviet Union would, at the appropriate moment, enter the war against Japan. The assurance had been repeated to President Roosevelt at Teheran. But at Yalta it appeared that there would be a price to pay. There the Russian leader demanded an understanding by which the United States and Britain were asked to agree that Russia should receive from China a free port, a naval base, and railway rights in Manchuria, in theory Chinese territory. The Russians were also to get the Kurile Islands, stretching eastward into the Pacific, and southern Sakhalin, then in the possession of Japan. To these terms, with slight modifications, Roosevelt acceded. He did so in a secret document, which was not communicated to his Secretary of State. Nor was he candid when, on his return from Yalta, he addressed the Congress with regard to what had taken place there. He made one of the very few secret deals in the history of the United States.

These events have been the subject of so much debate and criticism that they should be examined carefully. We must remember that Roosevelt had been told by his military advisers that Russian aid was essential to the victory over Japan. In effect, he was acting in the belief that an accord was necessary to save possibly thousands of American lives. He might also have argued that, whether he acceded or not to Stalin's demands, the Russians would have been in a position to take what they asked for (except for the Kuriles, which the Americans could have occupied). Though he could not know it at the time, the Chinese Nationalists, in their own later negotiation with the Kremlin, were to accept terms not very different from those discussed at Yalta, in the hope and with the assurance of Russian good will. But we must not forget the other side of the account. Russian assistance turned out not to be necessary; and though it is true that Russia could in any case have extorted from the Chinese the demands we have been analyzing, the fact remains that the President acted with doubtful constitutional propriety, and in a way contrary to American diplomatic tradition. We shall not judge him harshly, in view of the pressure under which he labored, but neither will we completely excuse his action.

At a later date, Yalta was to be the subject of bitter and partisan debate. Extravagant charges were made against the Roosevelt administration; it was alleged that the collapse of Nationalist China flowed from the engagements we have been analyzing; but the truth is far otherwise. As we shall see in a later chapter, internal disorganization and inefficiency, not any external decision, explains the failure of Chiang Kai-shek to maintain himself in the years following the war.

Before we turn from Yalta to the events which brought the war in the East to an end, we must say a word about two other matters: the death of President Roosevelt on 12 April 1945, and the drafting of the charter of the United Nations at San Francisco in the period immediately following his demise.

No criticism of detail ought to be allowed to blur the fact that Roosevelt was a great war leader. The national effort over which he presided was stupendous; armed forces of over eleven million were raised; miracles of production were performed; to an unusual degree industrial peace was maintained at home, and wage and price stability secured. The President's leadership is, of course, only one factor in these matters; but it was an important one. But this is not all. The President intervened in many significant military decisions (as Professor Robert Greenfield has shown); and, most notable among these, it was he who determined that the major effort should first be directed against Germany, and yet adequate support be given to the war in the Orient. It was he who, in the face of opposition from his military advisers, determined upon the North African campaign, as a way to bring American power to bear before forces could be gathered for the grand assault on the beaches of Normandy, and these decisions were of critical significance in the operation of the Grand Alliance. These matters, indeed, had a profound diplomatic as well as military import, and they should therefore be recorded in such a narrative as this.

There is one other major diplomatic-military decision of the President's that has been a matter of much discussion; the enunciation, at Casablanca, in the winter of 1943, of the doctrine of unconditional surrender. The declaration was not a mere impulse; we know that the matter was discussed with Churchill, and that the British Prime Minister referred the matter to his cabinet. But the President's critics have sometimes suggested that the principle may have contributed to the prolongation of the war and to the bitterness of resistance of the Axis powers. In dealing with such a question, we tread on the dangerous ground of hypothetical history; no one can really say what would have happened if events had been other than what they were. But, in the light of the historical record, it seems fair to say, with regard to the end of Italian resistance in 1943, that the doctrine of unconditional surrender had little impact; there *were* negotiations; indeed *some* confrontation and *some* discussion at the end of hostilities followed naturally from the eager desire of the Italians not only to get out of the war, but to protect themselves from German wrath, and to join the winning side; and the final result of the conversations that took place was to enlist the Italian government in the alliance against Hitler.

But what of Germany? Did the doctrine of "unconditional surrender" prolong the resistance of the regime in Berlin? It does not seem likely. Hitler, we may be reasonably sure, would, in any circumstances, have fought on to the finish; and his dramatic suicide in the bunker at Berlin gives us convincing evidence of the fact that with him it was either rule or ruin. But might not a more conciliatory position have strengthened the forces of underground opposition to the German tyrant, and brought about an internal collapse? It would be dangerous to dogmatize on such a matter; but it is significant that in the summer of 1944, a year and a half after the meeting at Casablanca, a far-reaching and extensive plot against the dictator was set in motion, and brought to the verge of success. It involved the assassination of Hitler himself; it failed because the bomb which was meant to annihilate the Fuehrer fell short of accomplishing this result; but the existence of the plot suggests that German patriots were not deterred from action by the President's declaration. As to the effect of the declaration on the end of the war with Japan, that is a matter to which we must later turn.

The death of Roosevelt, however, comes almost at the exact time that the great conference met at San Francisco to draft the charter of the United Nations. Congressional support for the general idea of the charter had been expressed some time before; and long conversations between the principal powers had already taken place before the conclave by the Golden Gate convened. The dream of Woodrow Wilson had not died; and the representatives of most of the peoples of the world met to invest it with some reality.

The structure of the organization that was set up at San Francisco was in many ways suggestive of the earlier structure of the League; there was, for example, to be an Assembly in which all the 'peace-loving' states of the world were to be represented; there was to be a Council, in which a special position was to be reserved to the great states, and two-year representation (based on election by the Assembly) given to the smaller ones; there was to be a Secretary-General to serve as the Executive Officer of the world organization; there was to be a system of trusteeships for undeveloped territories not unlike the mandatory system set up by the covenant of the League; there were to be collateral bodies to deal with specialized aspects of international affairs. The striking differences between the covenant and the charter were two: the covenant had dealt lightly with the question of military action for the maintenance of peace; the charter looked toward an international armed force. But what was here regarded as an advance was accompanied by what must be regarded as a retreat; the charter gave to the great powers an absolute veto over all matters not matters of procedure. This provision was adopted with the thorough concurrence of the American delegation; indeed, it was thought in many quarters that it was essential if the adhesion of the Senate of the United States was to be secured. How this was to operate in practice we shall see somewhat later in our narrative. It will suffice to say at this point that the charter was ratified by a vote of 89 to 22. Thus once more was born an international organism which expressed the aspirations of the peoples of the world for a more secure international order.

In the meantime the Japanese war moved toward a victorious conclusion. The Japanese navy had been largely destroyed; and the assault forces of the United States had advanced to within 400 miles of the main Japanese island. In July, the chiefs of the three great allies met at Potsdam. While the conference was in session the news arrived of the successful explosion of the atomic bomb at Alamagordo, New Mexico. On the 26th of the month Britain and the United States addressed to the Japanese government the Potsdam declaration, a solemn warning to Nippon. This declaration assured Japan that the West did not desire to enslave her, maintain the permanent occupation of the country, or root out her trade. It went on to say, however, that 'there must be eliminated for all time the authority and influence of those who have deceived and misled the people of Japan,' and that all conquests be stripped from her. 'We call upon the government of Japan,' it continued 'to proclaim now the unconditional surrender of all Japanese armed forces, and to provide proper and adequate assurance of good faith in such action. The alternative for Japan is prompt and utter destruction.'

This declaration was not accepted by the Japanese government. Brave men in the cabinet knew that the game was lost—notably the Japanese Foreign Minister Shigenori Togo. But Togo could not convince his colleagues. So it was that President Truman came to a momentous decision. Firm in his conviction that it was his responsibility to shorten the struggle, and save possibly hundreds of thousands of

American lives, he gave orders for the launching of the dread new weapon of war. On 6 August, a bomb was dropped on Hiroshima; 70,000 persons were killed, and many more exposed to radiation which might cause future disease and even death. Still the Japanese government hesitated to sue for peace. On the 9th a second bomb was dropped, this time on Nagasaki. On the 10th the Japanese admitted defeat. Yet their action was not unconditional. They were willing to accept the Potsdam declaration with the understanding that 'the said declaration does not comprise any demand which prejudices the prerogative of His Majesty as a Sovereign Ruler.' In other words, they demanded that they be allowed to keep their Emperor. Secretary of State Byrnes responded the next day. He did not demand the removal of the Emperor from the throne, but stipulated that 'the authority of the Emperor and the Japanese Government should be subject to the Supreme Commander of the Allied powers.' There followed a final reply from Tokyo that brought the war to an end. On 2 September 1945, on the battleship *Missouri* in Tokyo Bay, General MacArthur, surrounded by high army and navy dignitaries, formally received the Japanese surrender. His occupation of Japan followed.

Some historians have raised the question as to whether the war might not have been terminated sooner if the Tokyo government had been told at an earlier date that the Emperor would be left on his throne. The suggestion was made as early as May by some of the President's advisers—notably by one of the best informed, Joseph C. Crew, our former ambassador in Japan—and Secretary of War Stimson endorsed it in the first days of July. The question was discussed at Potsdam, and decided by Secretary Byrnes in the negative. Would a clear and early statement have shaken the position of the militarists who controlled the Japanese government? Like all hypothetical questions, no categorical answer can be given. But Doctor Herbert Feis who was in the State Department at the time, has analyzed the matter with great care in his book, *Japan Subdued*, as has Professor Butow in *The Surrender of Japan*. The answer which Feis gives to this inquiry is that the Japanese government came only very slowly to the acceptance of defeat, and that the most that can be said is that explicit warning of the portentous weapon might conceivably have had some effect at the time of the Potsdam declaration—but not earlier. Professor Butow takes a similar view.

The larger question, of course, is about the necessity for dropping the bomb at all. There is little question that Japan could, in due course, have been brought to her knees without the use of the new weapon. Says Dr. Feis:

There can hardly be a well-grounded dissent from the conclusion reached by the members of the U.S. Strategic Bombing Survey after their inspection of the condition to which Japan had been reduced by the Summer of 1945. From its studies of Japanese resources, military position and ruling politics, the Survey estimated 'that certainly prior to December 31, 1945, and in all probability prior to November 1, 1945, Japan would have surrendered even if the atomic bomb had not been dropped, even if Russia had not entered the war (as she did on August 9), and even if no invasion had been planned or contemplated.'

But to say this is by no means to say that the decision taken in August 1945 was not an intelligible, and a defensible, position. The extent of the prostration of Japan was not fully understood by the American authorities. As so often in practical affairs, the authoritative data were not there at the moment of decision. The prolongation of the war would have involved an uncounted number of American lives. It would have been a fearful ordeal for the Japanese. Even as it was, more lives were lost in the great American incendiary air raid on Tokyo in March 1945 than were killed at Hiroshima, and more damage was done. To quote Dr. Feis again,

Had the war continued, even greater groups of American bombing planes would have hovered over Japan, consuming their land and its people with blast and fire, leaving them no place to hide, no chance to rest, no hope of reprieve. A glance at the charts kept in the Headquarters of the U.S. Strategic Air Force at Guam, with its steeply ascending record of bombing flights during the summer of 1945 and scheduled for the next month or two, leaves visions of horror of which Hiroshima is only a local illustration.

It can well be argued that the surgical operation involved in the dropping of the bomb was preferable to the prolongation of the war, and this was not only from the American point of view, but with humane regard for the Japanese themselves. War is always brutal; war is passionate and violent; it develops its own momentum; it is only by seeking the means of avoiding it that we can spare humanity its horrors.

There is something more to be said. The men on whom rested the decision of 1945 were convinced of its necessity. The ultimate responsibility lay with the President, of course, but the decision was by no means his decision alone. As early as June, the question of the use of the bomb was discussed in an Interim Committee of Civilians appointed by the President. To this committee was added an advisory panel of scientists, some of the most eminent in the country, such men as James B. Conant, the president of Harvard University, and Robert Oppenheimer, one of the principal architects of the bomb itself. These men were all of the same mind; they rejected such alternative courses as an advance warning, or a demonstration of the power of the new weapon. Other scientists, it is true, took a different position, but the impressive fact is that men of the highest sense of responsibility and courage came to a clear conclusion. As for the statesmen, there was little doubt. 'I regarded the bomb as a military weapon, and never had any doubt that it should be used,' said Truman. 'The historic fact remains,' wrote Winston Churchill, 'that the decision whether or not to use the atomic bomb to compel the surrender of Japan was never even an issue. There was unanimous, automatic and unquestioned agreement around our table; nor did I ever hear the slightest suggestion that we should be otherwise.'

Of one other thing there can be no doubt. The invention of the nuclear weapon ushered in a new era in the history of foreign relations. Though the Americans would have had it otherwise, though a sincere effort was made in the period following the end of the war to bring about some understanding with regard to the limitation of the new instruments of war, what was really inaugurated was not only an arms competition on a hitherto unprecedented scale between the United States and the Soviet Union, but utterly new conditions within which the diplomacy of the future was to operate. The story of the years since 1945 is a story in which the policies of the American government are deeply involved with the fate of many lands. Isolationism, the gospel of the 'thirties, no longer had relevance; for better or worse, the United States stood forth as a world power in the widest sense of the term.

X   THE TRUMAN ADMINISTRATION

When General MacArthur signed the agreement with Japan on 2 September 1945, thus bringing the Second World War to an end, it is probable that most Americans looked forward to a period of international tranquillity, to what in an earlier generation Warren Harding had described as 'normalcy.' Their disposition in this regard was seen in the pressure for the lifting of the war controls; it was seen in the widespread belief that it was possible to live on terms of accord with the Soviet Union; it was seen above all in the proposal soon initiated and pressed in 1946 for the international control of the awesome weapon of war that had had so much to do with the termination of the conflict; it was seen in the widespread enthusiasm for the United Nations charter and the principles that it enunciated.

The question of atomic weapons deserves special attention. As early as November 1945, the United States, Great Britain, and Canada issued a three-power declaration in which they advocated the establishment of a United Nations Commission to make recommendations for the 'elimination from national armaments of atomic weapons and all other weapons adaptable to mass destruction.' Not much later the Russians agreed, and such a commission was set up. By June 1946 an American proposal had been framed for the establishment of an International Atomic Development Authority with wide powers. The United States agreed, if a system of control were set up, gradually to hand over its own supplies of weapons until, when the system was firmly established, the manufacture of atomic bombs would be forbidden and the entire stock destroyed.

In our present perspective, it is reasonably clear that such a proposal had little chance of acceptance by the Soviet Union. The Soviets themselves had initiated a program of atomic research, and probably chose from the beginning to develop this program in competition with the

United States, rather than concede to America, if only for a term of years, a superior position. The inborn suspicion of the foreigner that characterized Russian policy made it very difficult, if not impossible, for the Kremlin to accept the international controls that were, in the view of most of the world, the indispensable precondition for the internationalization of nuclear power. Though the Russian position was at times equivocal, the Soviet Union demanded the immediate destruction of atomic stock piles prior to the enforcement of any control, and a veto over any decision of the Security Council as to enforcement. Such proposals could not possibly be acceptable to the United States. The whole project thus broke down. Yet it must be a matter of pride to every American that in 1946 the United States was ready to surrender the favored position which it had attained in the international world, and to go further toward international control of arms than any nation had ever gone in the long history of mankind.

Yet the sharp division of feeling between the American government and the Kremlin is easy to understand. In all alliances, centrifugal tendencies assert themselves when the danger is over. In this case, doctrinal factors accentuated these tendencies. To Stalin and his comrades, the eventual world triumph of Communism was naturally a prime objective; in the attainment of this end, the use of Soviet power was justifiable whenever it was expedient; to the Americans, on the other hand, what was important was the restoration of Europe, the prosperous development of their own system, a world of peace and tranquillity. Indeed, the more clearly the Russian system came to be understood the more repulsive it seemed. To conservatives its economic theories were repugnant; to liberals its prostitution of the human mind to the purposes of the state, its rude suppression of dissent, its creed of violence were equally offensive. The clash of systems was to be foreseen.

The friction, as we have seen, began before the end of the war. The Russians, from their point of view, had some ground for complaint. The abrupt termination of lend-lease after the defeat of Germany, though required by law, was irritating to the Kremlin. The interest of the United States in Eastern Europe seemed an officious intrusion in the Russian security zone. The obvious determination of the American government to run the occupation of Japan as it chose was not calculated to be soothing to Stalin. The loan offered to Britain in the fall of 1945 seemed an act of partiality toward one ally that could hardly please the other. The visit of Churchill to America in the winter of 1946 and his speech at Fulton, Missouri, in which he urged the unity of the West, could hardly fail to be received with distrust in the Kremlin.

But the grievances on the other side were very real indeed. The great question was Germany. The Western powers, in their own interest, had no desire for a weakened Germany, or any disposition to carry the economic burdens of a German people denied the opportunity for recovery. The Russians not only plundered the eastern zone they occupied, but put forward fantastic demands for reparations, and kept talking of the internationalization of the great industrial district of the Ruhr. As time went on and it became clear that they could not get immense gains from the West, Stalin and Molotov, his foreign minister, obviously came to the conclusion that it was best to keep Germany disunited, to build up Communist strength in the zone that they controlled, and to go it alone. By September 1946, it was evident that understanding was impossible. In an important speech at Stuttgart, Secretary of State Byrnes demanded the early establishment of a provisional German government, and the abolition of the zones of occupation into which Germany had been divided at the time of the armistice. He also made it clear that the Americans intended to stay in Germany as long as the Russians did.

In the winter of 1947, the increasing tension between the Kremlin and the West was brought into even sharper focus. Since the end of the war Greece had been under British occupation. Under their aegis an election had been held, which established a right-wing government in power. In the meantime, either at Russian instigation or with Russian connivance, guerilla forces from the Communist states of Yugoslavia and Bulgaria engaged in constant fighting along the border. The Greeks themselves became discouraged, and what was worse, the British found the occupation a heavy burden. In February they indicated that they could no longer carry it. Would the United States step into the breach?

Of President Truman, to whom this appeal was directed, it could never be said that he lacked the capacity for decision. Little known when he acceded to the presidency in 1945, he gave a first impression, perhaps, of lack of certainty. But as time went on, his resolution and clarity of purpose became evident. Though he confronted a Congress in which his own party was a minority, he delivered before that body on 12 March a speech of the first importance. He demanded an appropriation of $400,000,000 for assistance to Greece and to Turkey, which was also the object of Russian pressure. In sweeping language he declared that the United States was ready to

help free peoples maintain their free institutions and their national integrity against aggressive movements that seek to impose on them totalitarian regimes. This is no more than a frank recognition that totalitarian regimes, imposed on free peoples, by direct or indirect aggression, undermine the foundations of international peace, and hence the security of the United States. I believe that it should be the policy of the United States to support free peoples that are resisting attempted subjugation by armed minorities or by outside pressures.

The Truman Doctrine, as it came to be called, like the Monroe Doctrine before it, and many other declarations of American policy, was framed in terms so wide as to be open to question, and to commit the United States beyond either its power or its interest. But on the concrete question the President had widespread support, although both houses of Congress were Republican. He was helped particularly by Senator Vandenberg of Michigan, a veteran Senator whose conversion from his previous isolationism was complete. Both Houses of Congress supported the bill by good majorities, the House by 287 to 107, the Senate by 67 to 23.

The temper of the country was further shown by what followed. In the winter of 1947 Europe suffered from severe economic distress. Here was a region of advanced technology and immense resources which might be lost to the forces of democracy if this distress grew. Here was a golden opportunity for the plotters of the Kremlin. But the danger was perceived. On 5 June, at the Harvard Commencement, Secretary of State Marshall (who had succeeded Byrnes in January) delivered an epoch-making speech in which he declared, 'it would be neither fitting nor efficacious for this Government to undertake to draw up unilaterally a program designed to place Europe on its feet economically,' but added that if Europe drew up such a program, the United States would provide 'its friendly aid' and 'later support for such a program so far as it may be practicable to do so.'

The results on both sides of the Atlantic were sensational. In Europe the Russians tried to block the plan. They compelled the Poles to refuse an invitation to discuss the matter with the ministers of other European states, and they forced the Czechoslovaks, who had accepted, to withdraw their acceptance. None the less the powers of Western Europe set up a Committee on Economic Co-operation, pledged themselves to co-operate in measures designed to open up the channels of international trade, and to assure fiscal sobriety, and in general responded in a spirit of high statesmanship to the American challenge. In America, a great campaign was started to educate the American public and to analyze the problem in terms of American responsibility. As in the case of Greco-Turkish aid, Senator Vandenberg and many other Republicans rallied to the support of the administration. Before the end of 1947, interim aid had been granted; in the spring of 1948 the first appropriations under the Marshall Plan (as the new policy was generally called) had passed both Houses of Congress by large majorities, in the House by a vote of 329 to 74, in the Senate by a vote of 69 to 17. No doubt the big vote was due in part to the mistakes made by the Kremlin. In February, with Russian encouragement, the Democratic government of Czechoslovakia had been overthrown, and a Communist regime put in its place. In the spring the bitter Communist opposition to the plan in France and Italy dramatized the issue for the American public. The challenge was made clear, and it was answered no less clearly.

The Marshall Plan lasted from 1948 to 1952. Over a four-year period, and excluding other assistance such as military aid, the program cost the United States over $13 billion. The sum seems staggering. But the gross national product of the United States in the single year 1948, when the plan went into operation, was $239 billion, and for the four years 1948-51 it was $1100 billion; in other words, little more than 1 per cent of the production of the American people was diverted to foreign aid. Moreover, the dollars advanced to European governments were, to a very substantial degree, spent in the United States. They served to stimulate the American economy as well as to revive the economy of the Old World. And the results were sensational. By 1952 industrial production for the Marshall Plan countries was 35 per cent over the prewar level, and agricultural production 10 per cent over prewar figures. Inflationary tendencies had been checked, budgets balanced, currencies brought under control, and machinery set up by which the European states could co-operate more effectively than ever before.

In the meantime a new challenge arose. The city of Berlin was under four-power occupation, but access to it was through the Russian zone of occupation. In the spring of 1948 the Russians cut off communications with Western Germany, virtually placing the former German capital under siege. The response of the American government, at first with some misgivings and then decisively, was to supply the city by air. The operation was a massive one. As much as 4000 tons a day was air-lifted into the city when the operation was at its peak. In May 1949 the Russians lifted the blockade, and normal intercourse was resumed.

But the Berlin air-lift was only one evidence of the changing temper in the United States. Once again Senator Vandenberg was the leader, at least in Congress. In April 1948 he introduced a resolution into the Senate directing the United States to promote 'association of the United States by constitutional process, with such regional and other collective security arrangements as are based on continuous and effective self-help and as affect its national security.' This resolution passed the Senate by 64 to 4. It was the augury of a diplomatic revolution, of a policy of alliance as opposed to a policy of independence.

So sweeping a commitment was naturally resisted by some elements of American public opinion. In particular, Henry Wallace, then Secretary of Commerce in the Truman administration, objected strenuously, and resigned his post in the government to become a candidate for President on a platform which sweepingly condemned the whole idea. But in the elections of 1948 Wallace polled a vote of only one million, and President Truman, who had already begun the negotiation of a treaty, was re-elected. There followed the document known as the Atlantic Pact, which bound the United States with the other eleven signatories, to the defense of Western Europe. This epoch-making document was signed in April; it was ratified by the Senate of the United States in July 1949, by the extraordinary vote of 82 to 13.

It was one thing to negotiate a treaty of alliance, and another thing to implement it. At first progress was slow. It was not until the middle of 1950, on the insistence of President Truman, that Mr. Eisenhower, at that time president of Columbia University, consented to become the commander in chief of the forces to be constituted under the new alliances. In 1951, to stimulate progress, the President dispatched four American divisions to Europe. There was sharp Congressional criticism of his action, but the Chief Executive was sustained by a vote of 69 to 21. The decision was a crucial one; indeed it may be stated categorically that since then the United States has been committed to the defense of Europe. Nothing in the present suggests that this support will be withdrawn, though the North Atlantic treaty has not met all the hopes of its founders.

The commitments made to Europe in the Truman years were

matched by diplomatic activity in the Far East. There the end of the war left the United States in occupation of Japan. And under the skillful administration of General MacArthur the country was rehabilitated, set upon a democratic course, strengthened by important social reforms, especially an important program of land distribution, and brought back into the family of nations by a wise peace treaty negotiated (over the opposition of the Soviet Union) in 1951.

A much more difficult question was that of China. During the war a determined effort had been made to strengthen the government of Chiang Kai-shek. But co-operation with the Nationalists, as we have said, turned out to be extremely difficult. The Nationalist leader quarreled violently with General Stilwell, the American commander in China; he withheld his best troops to check the growth of Communist power in northwestern China where the Reds were building up a strong regime with widespread peasant support; his government was often venal and corrupt; the government was utterly incapable of providing and carrying through a dynamic program of social reform. As early as 1944, almost a year before the end of the war, a well-informed American wrote, 'Communist growth has been almost geometric in its progression. From control of some 100,000 square kilometers with a population of a million and a half, they have expanded to about 850,000 kilometers with a population of 90 million. And they will continue to grow.'

Faced with this problem what was Washington to do? At the close of the war it strengthened Chiang's position by air-lifting Chinese troops to the principal cities of North China, by occupying the ports with American marines, by continuing the program of economic aid inaugurated before the war, and by delivering to the Nationalist government military supplies already in the country. Moreover, it offered to help the Generalissimo develop an armed force strong enough to establish and maintain internal peace.

What it could not do was to back the Nationalist leader in a full-scale war against the Communists. Such a course would have identified Chiang with an outside power and enabled the Reds to present themselves as the defenders of Chinese nationalism. Moreover, a costly campaign involving large numbers of American troops would retard demobilization at a time when public opinion was clamoring for the return of the soldiers. In addition to this, military aid to Chiang, to be effective, would have to be combined with a really attractive program of domestic reform, involving heavy financial commitments.

And this effort would have to be made in behalf of a government which seemed unable to grapple with its problems, which could not manage its currency, and which could not exercise effective control over its own forces, or even pay them regularly.

The alternative policy adopted, however, was almost equally unattractive, and, as the event proved, unrealistic as well. This policy was to try to bring about an accommodation between Chiang and Mao Tsetung, the Communist chieftain. In our present perspective it seems probable that it never had a real chance of success. The most hopeful moment was in 1946 when President Truman sent General Marshall to China to bring about an accommodation between the two factions. But after an initial period, the negotiations broke down. The Communists steadily improved their position in northern China; the morale of the Nationalist troops steadily deteriorated; they were cooped up in the towns while the Communists roamed the countryside. Despite substantial aid to Chiang from the United States in 1948, matters went from bad to worse; by the beginning of 1949 Peiping and Tientsin had fallen; by the end of May the Communists had entered Shanghai; before the year was out they had overrun south China, and the Nationalist leader had fled to Formosa. The rout was complete.

Despite the frustration of many Americans at the collapse of the Nationalist regime, the first impulse of the Truman administration was to 'wait for the dust to settle.' But before the President left office, a new series of events resulted in new commitments in the Far East that were to last for many years.

The country of Korea, at the close of the war, had been placed under Russian and American administration, the Russians occupying the area north of the thirty-eighth parallel, the Americans the area south of that line. It was hoped that this arrangement would be temporary; but the Russians set up a Communist regime in the north, while the Americans established a nominally democratic government in the south under President Syngman Rhee. In 1948 and 1949, respectively, the Russians and the Americans withdrew; but the Russians left a strong military government in the north, while the Americans had neglected to build similar strength in the south. On 25 June 1950 the North Koreans crossed the border in bald aggression against the Rhee regime.

At this moment, as it happened, the Russians were boycotting the Security Council of the United Nations, on the alleged ground that Communist China was not represented there. With American urging, and freed from the possibility of a Russian veto, the Council met at once, unanimously adopted a resolution stigmatizing the North Korean government as an aggressor, and called upon the members of the world organization to 'render every assistance in bringing about a restoration of peace.' The burden of supporting the charter fell, in all but full measure, upon the United States. American naval and ground forces, along with the gallant South Korean troops, bore the brunt of the struggle, directed by General MacArthur, who was in command in Japan. The initial phase of the conflict ended in the complete rout of the North Koreans. But by the end of October, the Chinese Communists entered the war. By this time, in conformity with a resolution of the Security Council, the American and South Korean forces had entered North Korea, and some units had even advanced to the Yalu River. But their lines had been overextended. Sweeping Chinese advances followed, and the war turned against the Americans.

What was to be done next? General MacArthur, the commander in the field, proposed a whole series of measures which he thought might bring the Chinese to terms. He wished to bomb the Chinese bases in Manchuria, blockade the coast of China, use Chinese Nationalist troops in Korea, encourage the Nationalists to invade the mainland, and give them logistical support in such operations. In short, he favored a very substantial extension of the war in order to achieve victory in Korea.

The Joint Chiefs of Staff in Washington, who were responsible for the military policies of the United States, had other ideas as to the proper course of action. For one thing, and most important, they feared that further commitments in the Far East would weaken the American position in Europe. The extension of the war into Manchuria might lead the Chinese to invoke their treaty of alliance with the Soviet Union, thus touching off a world war. At the least, it might lead to massive Soviet aid to the Chinese. There was a still stronger possibility that such action as the General recommended would put a severe strain upon the North Atlantic Treaty alliance, most of whose members were lukewarm about the Korean adventure. The measures MacArthur advocated, moreover, seemed inadequate to end the conflict. The blockading of China, it was argued, would mean little when China received most of her supplies by land; chances of effective use of the Nationalist troops on the mainland were small and the forces of Chiang Kai-shek, in all probability, would not be very welcome in

Korea. These considerations weighed heavily with the President's advisers in Washington.

MacArthur had been difficult to control from the outset. But now, just as the President was preparing to attempt negotiations in concert with the other nations participating in the war, the General issued a long and challenging statement addressed to the enemy. Declaring that the war proved that Communist China could never conquer Korea, and that an extension of the conflict would 'doom Red China to the risk of imminent military collapse,' he went on to commit himself to the unification of Korea. Moreover, he wrote to Congressman Martin, the Republican leader in the House of Representatives, sharply criticizing the administration's policy. 'It seems strangely difficult,' he wrote, 'to realize that here in Asia is where the Communist conspirators have elected to make their play for global conquest, and that we have joined the issue thus raised on the battlefield; that here we fight Europe's war with arms while the diplomats fight it with words; that if we lose the war to communism in Asia the fall of Europe in inevitable; win it and Europe most probably would avoid war and yet preserve freedom. As you point out, we must win. There is no substitute for victory.' After waiting ten days for some indication that the letter was confidential, Martin read it on the floor of the House of Representatives.

The President now acted decisively. He recalled MacArthur from his command, replacing him with General Matthew S. Ridgway. An explosion of feeling in the United States followed. MacArthur returned to the United States, and expounded his views before an excited session of the House and Senate. An indecisive Congressional inquiry followed. The administration stuck to its guns, and in the summer of 1951 armistice negotiations were opened with the Chinese Communists.

It is always possible to rewrite history by hypothesis. It is to be remembered, however, that Truman was following the counsel of his military advisers; and it seems equally certain that, as a result of popular demand for economy, and the budget-minded temper of Louis M. Johnson, the previous Secretary of War, the country was inadequately prepared for a greater effort than had been made. But wholly apart from this, the President was asserting a fundamental principle, the principle of the supremacy of the civil over the military authority. He was standing on his constitutional right—and duty—to make the ultimate decision in the field of military action. He acted with undoubted courage.

The Korean War was a fact of high historical significance. For one thing, we must reluctantly concede that it revealed the weakness in the doctrine of collective security, as laid down in the United Nation charter. Though some fourteen other nations collaborated with the United States in the war, 90 per cent of the burden was borne by the Americans and the South Koreans. Furthermore, the course of events made it clear that, had it not been for the chance Russian absence from the Security Council, no United Nations action would have been possible at all.

A second fact of great significance underlined by the struggle was the extreme difficulty of winning a land war on the continent of Asia. It is theoretically true that atomic weapons might have been used to lay waste much of China. But it remains to be proven that such a course would have brought the Communists to terms, and it would certainly have repelled a large part of the world.

Thirdly, the war resulted in a new commitment to Nationalist China. After the Nationalist collapse on the mainland, the disposition of the administration initially, as we have seen, was to wait for the dust to settle. But the outbreak of the Korean conflict changed the course of events. The administration, at the outset of the fighting, declared that it would not permit the Chinese Communists to invade Formosa; at the same time it interposed the Seventh Fleet between Formosa and the mainland and discouraged,—or virtually vetoed—any aggressive action by Chiang. This was, it is true, only a partial commitment; but it was an important step in that closer relationship with the Nationalist government which was to be forged in the next administration.

In the fourth place, the Korean war produced a violent explosion of partisan feeling. It threatened that bipartisan combination which had operated so effectively in the evolution of our European diplomacy. It was skillfully exploited by such men as Senator Joseph McCarthy, who took advantage of American frustration to wage an extensive and demagogic campaign against the Truman administration. Fortunately, however, when the Republicans came to nominate their candidate for President in the summer of 1952 they chose Dwight Eisenhower, who typified previous American policy toward Europe, and who was to follow through to a conclusion the armistice negotiations with the Chinese Communists which had been initiated by the Truman administration.

Looking back at the Truman years as a whole, we can hardly fail to regard them as of immense importance in shaping the foreign policy of the United States. The old isolationism was pretty well destroyed, and the United States assumed world responsibilities on an unprecedented scale. Gone was the notion that the United States could withdraw from the Old World, and safely cultivate its own garden in the American hemisphere. Gone was the idea—so long cherished by many Americans—that the American government could safely rely upon moral force to maintain its international position. Gone was the prejudice against the maintenance of adequate military strength. Men might still debate what the measure of that strength was to be, but on the principle of defense they were not very likely to differ.

The changes that we have just outlined were accompanied by important institutional changes. One of these was the creation of the National Security Council, provided for in the National Defense Act of 1947. This body, presided over by the President, also included the Vice President, the Secretary of Defense, the Director of the Office of Defense Mobilization, the Director of the Foreign Overseas Administration (the successor to the European Co-operation Administration). Others who might participate in its deliberations were the Secretary of the Treasury and the Secretary of State. Thus, for the first time, a single body co-ordinated military and diplomatic action.

A second important change was the establishment of the Central Intelligence Agency, also under the National Security Act of 1947. Down to the Second World War, the American government had no specialized instrument for the accumulation of accurate information in the field of foreign affairs. The ambassadors and consuls performed this function. But there are many things that ought to be known which do not fall within the range of these officers, as the period of the war amply demonstrated. The creation of this new agency (supplementing the Office of Strategic Services constituted during the war) was an important step toward the improvement of our foreign service mechanism. This is not to say that mistakes were not made. Indeed, the new office began ill, grossly misunderstanding the situation at the outset of the Korean War. But as time went on, it grew in efficiency, and, though errors were committed (as is inevitable in complex affairs), it has become an indispensable instrument of American foreign policy.

There is one more observation to be made with regard to the Truman period. It illustrates in a striking way the importance, in modern conditions, of a strong executive, who is also an experienced politician. President Truman possessed two transcendentally important qualities. He acted, in most instances, only after informing himself on the issues. He selected able men to provide him with this information, especially George Marshall and Dean Acheson, his secretaries of state. And then, when called upon to act, he acted with decision. Finally, he won from Congress a high degree of co-operation. Taking all these factors together, he must be rated as a very effective President of the United States.

XI THE EISENHOWER ADMINISTRATION

WHEN President Truman took office in 1945, or rather when the bomb exploded at Alamagordo, the United States occupied a position of undisputed power. But in 1949 the Russians detonated their own bomb. Temporarily, the American advantage might be thought to have been restored, when, in the same year, the United States set off a still more deadly weapon; but in 1953 the Russians, too, had this new weapon, the hydrogen bomb. While the exact measure of nuclear power in these first years is difficult to state, the long-range picture is clear. There was to exist a nuclear stalemate, which meant that the threat of the bomb on the one side was balanced by the threat of the bomb on the other. Did this mean that the new weapons would not be used at all? Not necessarily. They might still be used, in theory at least, against lesser powers. Their use might be considered if, somehow or other, the balance was destroyed, or means of defense discovered which nullified the employment of the weapon by the other side. Furthermore, the threat to use the bomb might be used as a means of deterrence, and if the threat failed, nuclear war might still occur. The dilemma before the governments which had the new weapon was a real one; to say that one would never use it was an invitation to weakness; to say that one would use it only as a weapon of retaliation was to give the advantage to the side which had the strongest conventional armaments, and the best strategic position; to threaten to use it was to take the chance that the threat would be defied, and retaliation result. How these questions were to be solved was no easy thing to discover; but at least it can be said that in the years that have elapsed since Alamagordo, no world disaster has occurred.

There is a second fact contemporaneous with the advent of the Eisenhower administration to power which must be mentioned before we embark upon the diplomatic narrative; in March 1953 the grim figure who had dominated Russia so long, Joseph Stalin, died. There followed a gradual transfer of power to a new and remarkable personality, Nikita Khrushchev. Immediately after the death of Stalin, Mr. K., as he came to be called, became the Secretary of the Communist Party with Malenkov as Premier; but by 1955 he had, by artful maneuvering, succeeded to the premiership, and by 1959, he had absorbed the post of President of the Soviet Union as well. To understand the events of the epoch, it is necessary to try to understand this complex and extraordinary man. In his domestic policy, Khrushchev stood for a less drastic policy than his predecessor; the role of the secret police was sharply curtailed; and there was, it appears, no such highly personalized power as that exercised by Stalin. In foreign affairs, his role was a complex one; bluster and cajolery were combined; the ultimate challenge, as we shall see, was avoided; but Communism continued to be a dynamic force; Communist propaganda was continued and extended; and Khrushchev himself in his travels sought to advance the Soviet system and to gain increased respect for his regime. We shall see what this meant in practice as the story proceeds.

But the first concern of the Eisenhower administration, when it took office in January 1953, was not with any direct challenge from Moscow. The first task was to end the war in Korea. Armistice negotiations, it will be remembered, had been initiated as early as the summer of 1951. But the Chinese prolonged the debates beyond the election of 1952, and even into the next administration. Indeed, for a time discussions were actually broken off. We do not know precisely what induced the Peking regime to come to terms in the summer of 1953; probably they were influenced by the fear that if they did not sign an agreement, the war would be resumed—and on an all-out basis. Shortly after the inauguration, John Foster Dulles, the new Secretary of State, intimated as much to Indian Prime Minister Nehru, and this intimation was no doubt transmitted to the Chinese Communist leaders. On 28 March, at any rate, they agreed to an exchange of sick and wounded prisoners; a month later they yielded on another point long in dispute, and showed willingness to accept an Indian proposal that prisoners taken by the United Nations forces, who did not wish to be repatriated (the vast majority), be put under the control of a neutral commission, that the Communists be given an opportunity of explaining to them why they ought to return, and that after ninety days, if they still held out, they should be given their freedom. On 27 July, the Chinese signed an armistice agreement—not a treaty of peace—that brought the war to an end.

The armistice, however, by no means meant the end of trouble for the United States in the Far East; the commitment to South Korea remained; and there was also the question of the proper attitude to be assumed toward the Chinese Nationalists, and toward the growing turmoil in southeast Asia.

It may be convenient to trace the first of these two questions to the end of the Eisenhower administration. The partisan attacks on the Truman administration for the 'loss of China' created special reasons for the Republicans when they returned to power to draw closer to Chiang; from the beginning President Eisenhower indicated his sympathy with the regime, and gave it economic aid; and on 2 December 1954 there was signed a treaty of alliance, which bound the two parties to assist each other in the event of an attack in the western Pacific area, and to meet the common danger 'in accordance with their constitutional processes.' Such a commitment might seem to make it possible for the Nationalists to provoke a war in which the United States would be bound to engage. To obviate this danger, a secret exchange of notes stipulated that the use of force by either party should be 'a matter of joint agreement, subject to action of an emergency character which is clearly an exercise of the inherent right of self-defense.'

The treaty posed another prickly question. Did it apply to the Nationalist-held islands of Quemoy and the Matsu group. The language of the agreement was cloudy. It declared that the pact applied to Formosa, the appendant islands of the Pescadores, and 'such other territories as may be determined by mutual agreement.'

There were, as always, those who criticized the commitments with Chiang, but the treaty was ratified by the Senate by an overwhelming vote, and it is in existence as this book goes to the press. It constituted another commitment in the Orient; what were its consequences?

Not, so far as our knowledge extends, very serious or embarrassing —though perhaps not necessary. The Communists continued to harass the forces on Formosa; and in January 1955 President Eisenhower asked for specific authority from Congress to employ American forces 'if necessary to assure the security of Formosa and the Pescadores.' After a brief debate, the House passed the desired resolution by 409 to 3, and the Senate by 85 to 3. Whether or not because of this action, the attacks of the Communists for a time subsided.

In 1958, however, after nearly four years of quiet, the Chinese Communists heavily bombarded Quemoy. The Eisenhower administration ordered the Seventh Fleet to convey supplies to the Nationalist troops on the island. It also provided them with 'side-winder' air-to-air rockets which enabled them to shoot down Communist planes with comparative ease. After two months of sharp activity the fighting died down; and up to the date of this printing it has not been resumed.

Besides its commitments to Chiang the Eisenhower administration made other commitments in the Far East. France possessed before the war a colonial empire in Southeast Asia, in the states of Laos, Cambodia, and Vietnam (Indochina). When the French returned at the end of the conflict, they soon found in the last of these states a condition of social unrest and rising nationalism, which compelled them to make heavy sacrifices in an effort to restore order. They were given large quantities of aid from the United States, on the principle that the advance of Communism was involved. In 1954, as their prospects darkened, President Eisenhower publicly advanced the 'falling domino' theory, which assumed that if Vietnam were lost, neighboring states would be toppled by Communism.

There was even some discussion at Washington of direct participation in the war. But the French tired of the struggle. A conference was called at Geneva. Shortly after it convened, the French sustained a severe defeat at Dien Bien Phu. Thus the way was paved for a compromise agreement with the Chinese Communists, who had, from the beginning, been assisting the Vietminh, as the rebels were called. Vietnam was divided into two parts, the Vietminh under Ho Chi Minh controlling the North, and a non-Communist group controlling the South. The United States refused to sign the agreement. In due course, indeed, it became the virtual protector of the southern regime. The commitment it made has lasted until the present day, and has imposed, as we all know, a heavy burden on the United States.

Yet Secretary Dulles was not yet content with the measures taken to protect the Orient against Communism. In 1954 he negotiated a treaty which created SEATO, the Southeast Asia Treaty Organization. Many of the most important Asian states, Burma, Ceylon, Indonesia, refused to sign, but the Philippines, Thailand, and Pakistan did so, and were joined by Australia, New Zealand, France and Great Britain. The treaty, more cautiously drawn than the Atlantic Pact, did not specifically provide for military action; in case of aggression in the area, the signatories agreed to meet the common danger in accordance with their constitutional practices and to 'confer in order to agree upon the measures to be taken for their common defense.' Although Cambodia and Laos were not signatories, since the Geneva agreement forbade them to enter into alliances, the treaty extended protection to them. It provided for individual and joint action 'to prevent and counter subversive activities directed from without.' Thus the United States found itself deeply committed in Southeast Asia.

Let us turn next to Latin America. During the period of the Second World War, partly due to the good-neighbor policy, and partly due to the economic advantages which came to the Latin American states as a consequence of the struggle, relations were good (except with Argentina, which became a center of Nazi intrigue and espionage). Even after the war, in the Rio Pact of 1947, the nations of the New World entered into an important collective security arrangement, providing for mutual consultation in case of external aggression and for common action against a law-breaking nation. But by the time the Eisenhower administration entered power, the bloom was off the rose. The preoccupation of the United States with Europe and Asia, the foreign aid extended to these areas, and in some instances a decline in the economic situation in Latin American states, produced a cooling of relations. Nor had President Eisenhower been long in office before a serious situation arose in Guatemala. The dictatorship of Jorge Ubico in that country had been overthrown in 1944. The liberal regime which succeeded it under President Arevalo afforded a cover for the increase of Communist influence. And the election of Arbenz in 1950 accentuated this tendency. An agrarian reform law was passed in 1952; when the judges of the Supreme Court sought to block the execution of the law, they were removed from office, and expropriations promptly followed. The United Fruit Company, which had important interests in the country, found these interests roughly handled. The American government sent a strong note of protest in April 1954.

But the American position met with very little sympathy when the Tenth Inter-American Conference convened at Caracas at about the same time. Hostility to foreign capital, and a dread of intervention by the United States, are often characteristic of the attitude of Latin American states. It is true that a resolution condemning 'the domination or control of the political institutions of any American States by the international communist movement' was passed without much difficulty (Guatemala alone objecting). But this did little to check the course of events. The Arbenz regime continued in its course. It drastically suspended civil liberties. It sought to stir up trouble in the neighboring state of Honduras among the banana workers. On 17 May news came that a shipload of arms from Poland was on the high seas, bound for a Guatemalan port. Matters came to a climax in June. Revolutionary forces directed against the Arbenz regime crossed the frontier from Honduras. The Arbenz government lost the support of the army, and after a few confused days, Castillo Armas, the leader of the revolt, became President.

There can be little question that the United States played a substantial role in these events. It was widely believed at the time that it had armed the forces used in the revolt. It is certain that the American ambassador at Guatemala City played an important part in the events immediately following Arbenz's resignation. Yet too great an emphasis on these facts blurs an important truth. It was the independent action of the armed forces that brought an end to the Communist-inclined regime. Had the army remained loyal, Armas could scarcely have succeeded. The essential element in the situation was the desertion of the Guatemalan military forces. And this desertion underlines and sustains the generalization that only when military disintegration occurs in a disordered state is the way paved for the triumph of Communism.

It is the difference in the military situation which explains, at least in part, the events which occurred in Cuba in 1959. In that rich and prosperous island the government of President Batista, which entered office in 1955, was increasingly corrupt and repressive. A revolt broke out in 1956, headed by a young revolutionary, Fidel Castro, who won much sympathy abroad, and, indeed in the United States, by his promises of a democratic regime and of social reform. The progress he made was slow, but in 1958 the American government, which had been supplying the Cuban government with arms, withdrew this support. The forces of Batista deteriorated in morale, and finally collapsed, and on 1 January 1959 Castro entered Havana in triumph. Once in office, he began to move rapidly toward the extreme left. The pledge to hold early elections was ignored; the Cuban patriots who had joined the revolution in the hope of a truly democratic regime were ousted from office; a flirtation began with the Soviet Union; and an agrarian reform law threatened the position of American investors in Cuba. The American administration began with moderate protests;

but sentiment in Congress became more and more hostile to the Cuban regime. Not long after the new regime was established, the Russian Deputy Mikoyan appeared in Havana, and an agreement was made to take five million tons of Cuban sugar, and for a grant of $100,000,000 to Castro; in May relations were resumed between Havana and the Kremlin; and confiscations of American property became more and more frequent and far-reaching. In June, acting under the authority of an act of Congress, President Eisenhower suspended the law which gave Cuban sugar a particularly favorable quota arrangement in the United States; in September Castro appeared at the meeting of the United Nations in New York, ostentatiously consorting with the Russians; and by the end of the year the administration had declared an embargo on trade with Cuba, which was almost total. In the meantime Cuban counter-revolutionaries had appeared in the United States; raids began to be staged on Cuba itself, and, as the nation was to learn later, encouragement was given to the anti-Castro Cubans in the form of support for their training exercises in Nicaragua and Guatemala, looking toward the possible invasion of the island. When President Eisenhower laid down his office, relations could hardly have been more strained; but the climax in this battle of ill-will was to come in the Kennedy administration.

That the administration was concerned at the events that had taken place in Cuba was natural enough; equally disturbing was the indifference of many Latin American governments to what was taking place there; and the hostile reception which Vice President Nixon had met with in the capitals of Venezuela and Peru on the occasion of a Latin American tour was another element that underlined the seriousness of the situation. The President and his advisers were therefore impelled to consider more seriously than before the dangers that lay in Latin American social and political unrest; and they took positive measures to combat it. One of these measures was the establishment of an Inter-American Development bank, a measure long advocated by some important Latin American statesmen. Another was an authorization bill for the extension of $600 million credits to the New World states; a third was encouragement to an international agreement to stabilize the price of coffee. Each one of these matters was important; but they could not alter the fact that for the first time in our history a Communist-oriented power had established itself in the New World, and that this power was seeking to undermine democratic institutions in other parts of the hemisphere.

The course of American diplomacy in Europe during the Eisenhower administration was marked, like its policy in Latin America, by all sorts of difficulties. At the close of the Truman administration, an ambitious plan had been drafted for the creation of an international European army, to which the six principal nations of Western Europe would contribute; this idea had been enthusiastically endorsed in the United States; but in France it met with much opposition, and the treaty which was involved was defeated in the French Parliament, after a long delay, in the summer of 1954. To this frustration, an answer appeared in the diplomacy of Anthony Eden, the British Foreign Secretary. A new arrangement was drafted, by which the West German state was admitted to NATO; the British and American governments agreed to keep troops in Europe so long as any danger of aggression from the Soviet Union existed; and to allay French fears of a rebirth of German militarism, the German republic was pledged not to manufacture atomic, chemical, or biological weapons, or long-range bomber aircraft, without the specific consent of the NATO commander and of two-thirds of the NATO council. The structure thus formed must be regarded as a constructive achievement.

The continuing distrust of the Soviet Union undoubtedly stimulated the agreement of 1954; but after it had been signed, and perhaps because it had been signed, the government of Premier Khrushchev attempted a brief courtship of the West. In a gesture which appeared to be propitiatory, it gave its consent to the liberation of Austria, which ever since the war had been under quadripartite occupation, and it further promoted a meeting of the heads of governments of Great Britain, France, the United States, and the Soviet Union in Geneva. Whatever may have been the emotions with which President Eisenhower responded to this invitation, the actual conversations which took place by the shores of Lake Leman were hardly satisfactory; the Western powers insisted on the unification of Germany (which implied, of course, free elections and the end of the Communist regime in East Germany); they put forward proposals for disarmament; but neither position was at all acceptable to the Russians, and the conference adjourned without any achievement whatever. Indeed, before another year had gone by, the tension between the West and the Soviet Union had become more severe than at any time since the air-lift to Berlin.

The crisis of 1956 centered on Egypt, where a revolutionary government under Colonel Nasser had come into power in 1954. From the outset, Colonel Nasser began a flirtation with the Kremlin. In order to arrest this drift toward Russian friendship, the United States, Great Britain, and the World Bank worked out an ambitious plan for the construction of a great dam at Aswan which would open large areas to cultivation and relieve the strain of Egypt's growing population. This proposal, however, met with no great enthusiasm in the American Congress, where Nasser was widely regarded as a trouble-maker, and a possible assailant on the neighboring state of Israel. Congress refused to authorize funds for the project, and just as the Egyptian government indicated its acceptance of the plan, Secretary Dulles in a curt note, indicated that the deal was off. The outraged Egyptian dictator retaliated by nationalizing the Suez Canal. A prolonged period of negotiation followed between Egypt and the Western governments. But in London and in Paris plans were matured behind the back of the United States to teach the upstart ruler a lesson. At the same time the Israelis, who had been viewing with apprehension the growth of Egyptian power, launched a 'preventive war' against Egypt. Two days later, London and Paris announced that they would land troops of their own to separate the two belligerents and to protect transit through the Canal. When the Security Council of the United Nations took cognizance of the question, the British and French vetoed a cease-fire resolution and pressed forward with their plans.

In response, ominous threats came from the Kremlin; in a note to the new Prime Minister of Britain, Eden, the Soviet President declared significantly that 'there are countries now which need not have sent a navy or air force to the coasts of Britain but could have used other means such as rocket technique.' Even more threatening was the statement that the Soviet Union was 'fully determined to apply force to crush aggressors and restore peace in the East.' In these circumstances the United States took an independent role. It denounced the action of its allies, the British and the French, and demanded the withdrawal of foreign forces from Egypt. Under severe pressure, the French and the British acceded; to the satisfaction of the supporters of the United Nations an international force was constituted to occupy the Gaza Strip, a point of maximum friction between Israel and Egypt, and the danger of war was averted. But not only did the Suez crisis temporarily weaken the bonds of the Western alliance; it gave the Russians an opportunity to interfere in the Middle East, and led, as we shall see, to further complications in the future.

It was also peculiarly ill-timed. It coincided with and diverted attention from the use of Soviet troops to maintain Russia's position in Hungary. There a revolution had overthrown the government and established a regime which demanded the right to withdraw from the Russian alliance and adopt a policy of neutrality. In the circumstances the West was powerless to support the new order. The Russians ruthlessly put down the revolt, treacherously seized and murdered its leader, and installed a new Communist regime in Budapest.

There can be little doubt, moreover, that the course of events in 1956 encouraged the Soviets to a more truculent tone. So, too, did other factors. In 1957, the Russians launched the first earth satellite. What this meant in terms of armed force was that they possessed the propulsive power sufficient to launch intercontinental ballistic missiles in orbit, and that the day might not be far off when such weapons would exist. In a statement intended to intimidate the West, Khrushchev declared at the end of 1957, 'I think I will not be revealing any military secret, if I tell you now that we have all the rockets we need.'

Nineteen-fifty-eight, indeed, was a year of increased tension. In the Middle East the Russians continued active. When the United States, at the request of the Lebanese government, landed troops in that little state to protect it against an internal convulsion, ominous mutterings came from the Kremlin. Toward the end of the year a new note of menace appeared. The Kremlin demanded that the Western powers evacuate their sectors of Berlin, which would then become a free city. It declared that if the West refused its proposal it would turn over control of the traffic to Berlin to the East German government, which was, of course, a puppet government the West refused to recognize. It gave the NATO powers six months to meet these terms.

In the face of these demands, as had happened many times before, the democracies drew together. The United States, the four great Western European powers, and the NATO Council all promptly condemned the Soviet attitude, made it clear that they would maintain their right to remain in Berlin, and declared that they could not consent to negotiate in the face of an ultimatum or time limit. Confronted with this situation, the Kremlin modified its tone; in answer to the statement of the West it indicated a willingness to discuss the Berlin problem and cognate issues in a meeting of the heads of states. The year 1959 was largely taken up with preparations for this meeting. In the course of these negotiations Premier Khrushchev himself came to the United States, held extended conversations with the President at Washington, and at the President's guest house at Camp David. Shortly after, the Chief Executive was invited to visit Moscow and plans were laid for a conference at Geneva.

The increased tempo of friendly exchanges between Russia and the United States suggested in the spring of 1960, at any rate to those of an optimistic cast of mind, that some kind of agreement could be arrived at between the two states. Yet neither one had conceded anything in concrete terms, and both, in fact, reiterated their previous stands. A speech by Secretary Herter, who took over the State Department after Dulles's death in February 1958, and another by Under Secretary Dillon, reiterated the American determination to stand fast on the question of Berlin. Khrushchev replied with an inflammatory discourse, reiterating his threat to transfer control of the routes to Berlin to the East German government if no agreement was reached with the West. He added that any attempt to supply Berlin by force would meet with resistance.

Then came a dramatic incident which shook the proposed conference to its foundations. On 1 May 1960, an unarmed American reconnaissance plane (U-2) was brought down at Sverdlovsk, 1200 miles within Russian territory, and its pilot taken prisoner. The world learned that through aerial operations the United States had gained extensive knowledge of Russian military sites, and much other useful information as well. In a radio speech to the Russian people, Khrushchev described what had happened, and denounced the United States. After a period of confusion, which only complicated the embarrassments of the situation, President Eisenhower and Secretary Herter made statements accepting responsibility for the plane and other similar flights over Russia, and Herter at least seemed to say that these flights would continue if American security so required. At the opening of the conference, which had now convened in Paris, the Russian Premier made the most of this; he demanded an apology from the President, refused to be propitiated by assurances that the flights had been suspended, vehemently castigated the Americans for bad faith, and finally broke up the conference. His action destroyed all hopes of an agreement and also discredited the whole concept of negotiation at the summit. In addition, the Russian Premier came to the meeting of the United Nations Assembly in New York at the end of the year, and in a display of boorishness without parallel, again sought to rally opinion against the United States.

A new source of friction developed in these months in the Congo. On 20 June the Congo had been liberated from Belgian rule and had become an independent state. In the confused situation that resulted, the Russians took sides with those Congolese elements most unfriendly to the West, and bitterly opposed the sending of United Nations forces to the new republic to maintain order and assist in the establishment of a firm government. The capacity of the Kremlin for trouble-making must have seemed endless to the harried statesmen in Washington.

What, in the broader view, is the judgment on the years of the Eisenhower administration? The first and most important consideration is that the commitments which had been made with regard to Europe were fully maintained. The defense of the West had become, one may fairly say, an integral part of American policy. In the operation of this program, there were, however, as we have seen, numerous difficulties. The harmony of the alliance was badly strained by the events of 1956, and by the brief Anglo-French occupation of the Suez Canal zone. The members of NATO were slow in meeting their commitments, partly because the view was widely held in Europe that the Russian position was one of bluster, and that in the face of a resolute stand, there was little danger that war would erupt. This is not to say that substantial forces had not been raised, and that the military power of the West had not greatly increased since 1953. But the critical question of the use of nuclear power, and in whose hands would rest the decision to use such power, had never really been decided, and in France, at any rate, with the advent of General de Gaulle to the presidency in 1959, there were signs of restlessness with regard to the distribution of power within the alliance itself.

Regarding the Orient and the Middle East, it is necessary to underline a fact already noted. The commitments of the United States had been substantially extended. In 1953 we had no alliances with any Eastern power, with the exception of a Tripartite Security Treaty with Australia and New Zealand, and a commitment to the defense of Japan, incorporated in the treaty of 1951. In 1961, we were bound in an alliance with Nationalist China, with South Korea, with Thailand, and were supporting with economic and military aid the native government in South Vietnam. We had also become more deeply involved in the Middle East. There we did not actually join the so-called Baghdad pact, signed by Great Britain, Turkey, Iran, Iraq, and Pakistan. But we smiled upon its operations, and in a message to Congress of 5 January 1957, the President requested authorization 'to employ the Armed Forces of the United States as he deems necessary to secure and protect the territorial integrity and political independence of any . . . nation or group of nations requesting such aid against overt aggression from any nation controlled by international communism.' The resolution in support of the President's request, though slightly modified in language, was passed unanimously in the House, and in the Senate by 72 to 19.

The complexities of the American diplomatic position were further increased by the establishment in Cuba of the first Communist-oriented government in the New World (save for the brief episode of the Arbenz regime in Guatemala). The tone of Fidel Castro was becoming more strident as the Eisenhower administration drew to a close, and the Cuban connection with Moscow more intimate. When President Kennedy took office in January of 1961, he faced problems of a variety and significance hardly paralleled in the history of the United States. We shall see in the next chapter how these problems were faced in the years from 1961 to 1965.

THE problems faced by the Kennedy administration when it entered office were as varied as they were portentous. But there was one matter which loomed above all others—the question of Cuba.

It seems likely that the Russian Premier, in no very amiable mood after the breakdown of the Paris conference in 1960, was disposed from the outset to test the mettle of the new President. And, as matters went at the beginning, it is comprehensible that he formed no very favorable opinion of the new executive. In April 1961 occurred the disastrous episode which has been known as the Bay of Pigs. For some time, as we have seen, Cuban refugees, with the tacit encouragement of the American government and with some assistance from the Central Intelligence Agency, had been preparing for an invasion of Cuba and the overthrow of the Cuban dictator. In April, they were conducted to the shores of Cuba by American naval vessels and then left to carry on their offensive action without effective support from the United States. The result was a complete fiasco. In foreign affairs, it is often the case that the middle course is the least safe; one must make a choice between two sharp alternatives. The Administration, by its halfhearted action got the worst of both worlds, and the blow to American prestige was a real one. No doubt it had its effect on the mood of the Kremlin. When President Kennedy met Chairman Khrushchev at Vienna in June, the meeting was an unfruitful one, and presented, as the President said, a 'somber' picture of the future.

The arrogance of the Kremlin was perhaps fortified by the events which followed. In August the East German government took the world by surprise by erecting a wall between East and West Berlin, thus checking the flood of refugees seeking freedom in the West. The NATO powers were unready to take decisive action; they contented themselves with no more than a formal protest. It is true that our forces in Europe were reinforced and the Vice President was sent to the former German capital to assure the West Berliners that the United States had no intention of abandoning them. But as in the case of the Cuban episode, the net effect was not reassuring.

In the autumn the Kremlin gave a new demonstration of militant purpose. Since the end of 1959 both the United States and the Soviet Union had abstained from nuclear tests in the atmosphere. But in September, the moratorium was rudely broken, and massive nuclear explosions again took place in Russia. A personal appeal by the President to suspend further tests was scornfully rejected.

All these things served only as a prelude to an act of duplicity and of defiance which had had no parallel even in the trying years just passed. The Russian government entered into an agreement with the government of Fidel Castro to install in Cuba missile sites, missiles, and bombers, from which a large part of the United States and northern South America could be directly menaced. In the execution of this maneuver it operated clandestinely; publicly it insisted that the only measures which it was taking to assist Cuba were purely defensive in character and declared that its own nuclear weapons were so powerful that there was no need of installing missiles in the New World. Mr. Gromyko, Russia's foreign minister, even sought to mislead President Kennedy at a meeting in October. By virtue of the remarkable aerial reconnaissance which the Americans exercised over Cuba, some knowledge of what was intended penetrated to Washington. As early as 13 September the President stated that if the safety of the country were threatened, his government would do all that was necessary to protect its own security and that of its allies. Congress passed resolutions to the same effect. On 2 October, the Organization of American States also sounded the alarm. The administration moved cautiously, however. Knowing well the gravity of the crisis, it was determined to have a solid basis of fact on which to act. By 14 October, it was clear that a deadly peril was near. Even then there were delays and new consultations. Finally, on 22 October, at seven o'clock in the evening, President Kennedy electrified the nation in a television address. Calling attention to Russian duplicity, he declared that 'this secret, swift and extraordinary build-up of Communist missiles . . . this sudden clandestine decision to station for the first time strategic weapons outside of Soviet soil—is a deliberately provocative and unjustified change in the status quo which cannot be accepted by this country if our courage and our commitments are ever to be trusted by either friend or foe.' He followed up this pronouncement by declaring a quarantine, by which ships of the American navy were directed to turn back vessels bound for Cuba with offensive weapons; he demanded removal of the Russian missiles and bombers already in Cuba, and an international inspection to verify this removal; he directed the armed forces to be prepared for all eventualities. In the sharpest language he declared, 'It shall be the policy of this nation to regard any nuclear weapon launched from Cuba against any nation in this hemisphere as an attack by the Soviet Union on the United States, requiring a full retaliatory response upon the Soviet Union.' Five hectic days followed. The Organization of American States on 23 October endorsed the position of the President. On the same day, in a powerful speech, Adlai Stevenson, the American ambassador at the United Nations, indicted the Russian government before the Security Council. On 25 October, at a second meeting, he directly challenged the Russian member of the Council, Mr. Zorin, either to affirm or deny the presence of missiles in Cuba. 'You can answer "yes" or "no",' he declared. 'Don't wait for the translation. You have denied that they exist—and I want to know whether I have understood you correctly. I am prepared to wait for my answer until hell freezes over, if that is your decision. I am also prepared to present the evidence in this room.' The Russian shuffled and evaded. On 28 October, however, Khrushchev yielded. He agreed to remove from Cuba the missiles of which the American complained, and to destroy the launching sites. He also agreed to remove the substantial number of bombers which the Russians had placed in Cuba. The crisis was over.

The administration did not gain everything that it had demanded. With regard to international inspection on the ground to verify the removal of the weapons, Castro took a defiant stand from which he could not be moved. But the essential point had been made. By keeping Cuba under aerial surveillance, the administration could rest assured that the peril had been averted. Ships bearing the missile weapons out of Cuba were subjected to search, and their contents verified. In due course the Russians fulfilled their engagements with regard to the bombers, and even withdrew by far the larger part of such troops as they had in Cuba.

The events of 22 October, and the days that followed, are very significant. We cannot measure them, of course, in the long perspective. But we can relate them to what followed. There can be little question that what followed was a release of the tension between the United

States and the Soviet Union. For example, a 'hot line' was established between Washington and Moscow to permit direct communication should new tension develop. The President and the Premier launched a substantial private correspondence, which must have been educational for both. More important than either of these things was the fact that the Russians, who had long resisted any agreement on nuclear testing, now agreed to a treaty forbidding such tests on land, on sea, and in the air, and the treaty incorporating this agreement was ratified by the Senate of the United States by the decisive vote of 79 to 19. An agreement with regard to missiles in outer space was reached. In the short perspective that we have on these events, the President's stand on Cuba appears to be one of the most courageous and influential ever taken by a chief executive of the United States.

We must not, of course, exaggerate. Nobody knows better than the diplomatic historian how dim must be the view of the future. The complexity of international politics in itself forbids a confident prediction for the years ahead. The death or removal of a statesman (Khrushchev, for example), a change in the public mood (of which we have had many illustrations in the course of this narrative), an economic depression in one country or a revolution in another, all these can present the spectrum of international politics in a new guise. We have already seen the oscillations of Russian policy. Nothing suggests that a new period of militancy may not at some time arrive; nothing suggests that the United States can cease to be on its guard.

Yet there are certain factors with regard to Russia which may reasonably be brought into the account as this narrative draws toward its close. To a degree, at least, the Soviet Union is losing its revolutionary character. The necessity for internal economic improvement presses upon the politicians in the Kremlin. The multiplying contacts with the outside world have had their effect in diminishing Communist fanaticism. One wonders what was the impression on Khrushchev as he saw the automobiles pouring down Park Avenue when he visited New York and the United Nations in 1959 and 1960, or when he saw the 'tall corn' growing in Iowa on the farm of Roswell Garst. More and more, Russians are becoming aware of the gigantic economic achievement of the West, and this awareness can, in the long run, hardly fail to have its effect on the foreign policy of the nation. We can go further. In speech after speech, particularly in recent years, the Russian Premier spoke of the folly of nuclear warfare, and of the perils of nuclear devastation. This, of course, may have been intended to terrify others; but it also reveals the fact, underlined by the Cuban crisis, that the Kremlin has no disposition to press so far in its policies as to provoke a new crisis like that of October 1962.

There is still another element in the equation when one comes to assess Russian policy at the present time. Many have become aware of Russia's quarrel with China, and of the restlessness and striving for independence of its satellites. The breach with China has been long in the making. In a brief review such as this, it is impossible to analyze the subject in detail. But several facts must be noted. As early as 1959 the Russian technicians who had been sent to China were returning home. Russian economic aid to the Chinese People's Republic has been ebbing away. The drastic policies of Mao Tse-tung and his colleagues in the economic sphere have met with no approval in Moscow. The exchange of insults has become more and more bitter; the divergence of policy more and more marked. We should not exaggerate the importance of the rift; but some months before his fall, Khrushchev warned Peking that it could not count on unconditional support if it pursued aggressive policies in the Orient. And the Russian-Chinese quarrel naturally permits more freedom of action to the United States in the Far East.

The situation which exists between Russia and the states of Eastern Europe has also altered. Yugoslavia, a Communist state, declared its independence of the Kremlin as early as 1948. While the views of Marshal Tito often run counter to the American position, he is no slave of the Soviet Union. The events of 1956 in Poland and Hungary have also had their impact. The Poles still have a Communist government. But they now grant an uneasy toleration to the Catholic Church and, like Yugoslavia, they have virtually ceased to support the collectivization of agriculture. The regime installed in Hungary by Russian bayonets after the revolt of that year has proven remarkably moderate in its attitudes. Finally, the Rumanians have declined to be incorporated in an East European economic bloc and are extending their trade relations with the West. None of these events should be given an exaggerated importance; but they illustrate the centrifugal tendencies that beset all alliances when they are not united by a common peril.

It is fair to say, of course, that a similar process has beset the great alliance of the West. A great dream lay behind American policy of the 'fifties, the development of a Western Europe united by close economic ties, and by a close military association. On the economic side, for a time, things went favorably. The establishment of the Iron and Coal Community, comprising France, Germany, Italy, and Belgium, the Netherlands, and Luxembourg (the so-called Benelux states), was a favorable start. The union of the same states in what was called the Common Market seemed also to be a happy augury for the future. But today there are several questions to be asked. The sharp refusal of General de Gaulle to admit the British to the Common Market, a veto permitted by the terms of the agreement, was a disappointment to Washington. In 1962 the Kennedy administration secured from Congress a reciprocal trade act which held out hopes of further lowering of tariff barriers among the states of the West. But as yet nothing has been done to implement this act. The question must be raised (it cannot be answered) as to whether the Common Market will become exclusive in its policies, or will be the prelude to wider understandings. On the military side, the international army project of 1952 was, as we have seen, defeated by French opposition. The new arrangements brought about in 1954 have resulted in some strengthening of NATO, but difficult questions remain. The most difficult turn upon the matter of nuclear power. For most of the members of the alliance the American nuclear umbrella is looked upon as a fundamental measure of protection, though from time to time misgivings are expressed, particularly in France. But General de Gaulle, that extraordinary statesman who has swayed the destinies of France since 1959, insists upon some measure of nuclear power for France, on the hypothesis that no European state can be certain of American support when and if its interests are threatened. The putting forward of this hypothesis, so characteristic of the logic of the French mind, hardly seems calculated to make American support more certain; to distrust the loyalty of an ally is hardly the way to fortify that loyalty. But even if we discount the effect of French action, even if we bear with patience the other obstacles which the great Frenchman has placed in the path of the alliance, there is a central question: shall the unleashing of nuclear power be based upon the sole decision of the United States, or shall it be the result of a collective decision? A satisfactory answer to this vexing question has not yet been discovered.

The forces operating to weaken the system of alliances represented by NATO and, on the Russian side, by the Warsaw Pact, are not to be thought of as presaging the collapse of the whole system. When genuine danger threatens in Europe, our European allies have spoken with one voice. But they illustrate a more general tendency, the tendency toward neutralism, and the disposition of the uncommitted states to remain uncommitted, so far as the two great giants are concerned. This tendency has been evident for some time, but it seems to be growing stronger. In Asia, for example, the Indian government has avoided any military tie with the West. The revolutionary government of Egypt skillfully plays upon the rivalry of Washington and the Kremlin to get advantages from both sides. The new states of Africa, and there are many of them, have no desire to become the instruments of either Russian or American policy. Americans, in the past, were disposed to believe that he who was not for us was against us. It will be quite impossible as a practical matter to take this position in the years ahead.

The thoughts just raised suggest another question of great significance. What is to be American policy with regard to the giving of assistance to states emerging from colonial status, desirous of expanding their economies and of broadening the basis of their economic life? The matter is discussed every year when the administration puts forward its plans for economic aid, and asks the Congress to implement such plans. All kinds of problems arise. Shall aid be given only to those states which, like the countries of Europe at the time of the Marshall Plan, set an example of balanced budgets, of governmental rectitude, and of common association for the improvement of their economic life? Or shall less exacting tests be demanded, in the hope that some good will come out of these contributions, and that the image of the United States will be improved in the nations which are the recipients of assistance? The answer that has been given to this question in practice is to give the bulk of the aid to a few states, but to grant small amounts to many. Those who oppose the whole adventure call attention to the fact that without a great internal effort external aid may be wasted, and that in the last analysis no nation can make substantial progress unless its own governmental processes are administered intelligently and in an orderly manner. Those who take the opposite view call attention to the dangers of neglect, to the possibilities of the establishment of regimes unfriendly to the United States, and to the hope that small advances may make a large difference, and have a multiplying effect. Whatever American policy is to be in the future (and its broad lines seem at the moment to have been established), several facts not always noted ought to be pointed out. The amount of aid granted in recent years amounts to little more than one-half of 1 per cent of the gross national product. Excluding military aid, which directly relates to the security of the United States, the amount is nearer one-third. Of this a substantial part is expended in the United States, and may be thought of therefore as contributing to the activity of the American economy.

In this summary of American foreign policy, there are three other questions about which something should be said. One is that of our foreign policy in Asia; the second is that of our policy in Latin America; and the third is that of the American attitude toward the United Nations.

With regard to the first, one fact is undeniable, and deserves to be repeated. We have binding commitments in the Orient, to Japan, to Nationalist China, to South Korea, and to the government of South Vietnam. How stands the account with regard to these commitments today?

With regard to Japan, despite an underground agitation which has sometimes been embarrassing to us (as for example when President Eisenhower was compelled to forgo a visit to Tokyo in view of leftist agitation there), the present position is not an uncomfortable one. Japan is undergoing a period of great prosperity; part of this prosperity is connected with the generous tariff policies of the United States; and the danger of an attack on Japan by any other power seems, as matters stand, remote. The present situation on Taipei is, on the whole, favorable. The Chinese Nationalists began ill on that island, and there was a substantial revolt there in 1947. But the government of General Chiang has, on the whole, whatever its authoritarian tendencies, materially advanced the prosperity of the island. The possibility of an attack from the mainland is largely to be discounted, and the massive naval power of the United States virtually guarantees the area against invasion. What will happen when the eighty-year-old Chiang passes from the scene, however, it is quite impossible to say.

The cases of South Korea and of South Vietnam present a different kind of problem. The United States learned in 1950 and 1951 the severe costs of a war on the Asian mainland. Preponderant American opinion is not at all inclined to undertake the experiment again. Whether the regimes at Seoul and Saigon can, with other types of aid, sustain themselves, whether they will fall victims to internal decay, or even succumb to the blandishments of the regimes to the North, is not a matter on which any confident judgment can be made. The future in this regard is bound to be obscure.

To discuss these matters inevitably raises the question of Communist China. There is a substantial body of unofficial opinion in the United States which affects to believe that recognition should be accorded to the regime in Peking, and that it should be invited to enter the United Nations. Such a view, whether at some time in the future it may be acceptable or not, fails, as matters stand today, to take account of some important realities. The American people suffered a traumatic experience in their war with the Chinese Communists in Korea. The armistice that ended the war was systematically violated by the Chinese, and hostilities had hardly ended in Korea when the Peking government began to encourage revolt in Vietnam. The question of recognition, moreover, has political overtones. We may be very certain that there would be violent opposition on the part of many Republicans in Congress if the administration began to flirt with the government of Mao Tse-tung. There have been indications, from time to time, that a solution might be found to the problem by the creation of two Chinas, each enjoying recognition, and each admitted to the United Nations. But there is not the slightest reason for supposing that the Communists would accept such an idea. There is every sign, indeed, that they are militantly opposed to it. Nor is it easy to see how General Chiang Kai-shek could be brought to acquiesce in any such arrangements. It is sometimes said that the United States would be much embarrassed by a vote in the United Nations to admit the Peking government. But on what terms will the question be phrased? The matter is full of legal and diplomatic perplexities. The cautious historian will utter no judgment on the matter.

It is quite another question whether a way ought to be found to bring peace to the Far East through an international conference to which the Chinese Communists would be invited. This matter has some relevance, since the French government of General de Gaulle has recognized the Communist regime, on the hypothesis that the questions of Southeast Asia can only be settled with its collaboration, and that any other course in Vietnam means a prolonged and wasting struggle. The possibility of a negotiated settlement ought not to be ruled out.

Our relations with Latin America present a different set of problems. While the matter can be given an exaggerated importance, it is probably true that in the years immediately following the Second World War, the diplomacy of the United States tended to concentrate on Europe and Asia, and assigned a lesser importance to the states of the New World. But the revolution in Cuba marked the end of this situation, and the Kennedy administration launched a program with the name of the Alliance for Progress, which is still in effect today. The central question posed is whether the Latin American states can achieve a measure of social and economic progress, without undergoing violent social change or succumbing to the wiles of international Communism. There are certainly centers of discontent in many of these states. The gross social inequalities which exist in many of them, perhaps one should say most of them, undeniably suggest the possibility of an explosion. The violent nationalism which is characteristic of the era, in virtually every part of the globe, affords a breeding ground for hostility to the United States. The disturbances which broke out in Lima and Caracas at the time of Vice President Nixon's visit to Peru and Venezuela were an illustration of the dangers that existed. And more recently, the events in Panama have underlined the intensity of nationalistic sentiment to which demagogues and Communists so easily make appeal. Of course the central problem is Cuba. There has been little sentiment in the United States for armed intervention. Such intervention would, of course, run counter to the engagements taken by the United States not to intervene in the domestic affairs of any American state, and would create great resentment in many quarters in Latin America. The American government has embargoed almost all forms of trade with Cuba, and put many obstacles in the way of Cuba's trade with other nations. It has secured increasing support from the other New World states, which in 1962 excluded Cuba from the Organization of American States and agreed to an embargo on shipments to the island. In 1964 all the Latin American states but Mexico had broken relations with Havana. It must be doubtful, however, whether measures of this kind will succeed in overthrowing Castro. Though the Cuban economy has much deteriorated, it is by no means certain that the economic difficulties will lead to a counterrevolution. In a sense, they may strengthen the nationalistic sentiments which sustain the regime. It is best to abstain from prophecy.

One of the striking developments of the last few years, as has already been indicated, is United States concern with the economic and social progress of the Americas. The institution of the Inter-American

Bank was followed during the Kennedy administration by the program known as the Alliance for Progress. The Congress of the United States appropriated over $3 billion to implement this program, a committee of experts has been appointed to analyze the problems to which it gives rise, and a number of states have drawn up plans of action which await implementation. It seems right to say that up to date the results have not been sensational. Inflation has prevented the full success of the experiment in some of the states. The shortage of technical experts presents another obstacle. But there are other difficulties which lie deeper. Even by the most optimistic view, the economic development of Latin American must depend upon private capital, native or foreign. And here progress is discouragingly slow. On the other hand, there are some things that private capital cannot do. The aid program has a positive value in stimulating those projects of public improvement and of public education on which the progress of the community in large measure depends. And the effect of such aid may prove to be cumulative. At any rate, though all kinds of foreign aid have met with much opposition in Congress, the last Congressional appropriations seem to show that the sentiment of the country is still in favor of grants of the kind that have been made in the past, while increasingly demanding that such grants shall be prudently administered.

A problem which constantly confronts the United States in dealing with the southern republics is that of how to deal with regimes which are not democratic in spirit, and which violate the constitutional forms of these republics themselves. The problem is not a simple one. No doubt the coddling or flattering of odiously dictatorial regimes (which has sometimes been done in the past) ought to be avoided. But, at the other end of the spectrum, the policy of refusal to recognize regimes which come into power by force presents many difficulties. Historically, it has rarely succeeded. It sometimes operates to strengthen the dictator by permitting him to appeal to national sentiment against outside interference. And it runs counter to the feelings of many Latin Americans as well. But perhaps the best way to view the question is to put the persuasive influence of the United States behind a return to constitutional forms wherever possible, and to encourage existing regimes of whatever nature to initiate programs of social and economic reform. Such a policy is not always easy to carry out in practice; but the old-fashioned military dictatorships seem to be less common in most of Latin America, and military governments, when they take office, seem more disposed to prepare the way for more democratic regimes.

At any rate, it is necessary to take account of the nature of Latin American politics, and not to imagine that we can remake the other New World states in our own image. In a famous debate in the House of Commons, turning on the question of association with Admiral Darlan, the Vice Premier of the French Petainist regime during the Second World War, Winston Churchill justified the relationship on the ground that the French military organization was highly hierarchical, and that dealing with Darlan immensely facilitated the invasion of North Africa by the British and Americans in the fall of 1942. 'I entreat the members of the House,' he declared, 'to remember that God in His infinite wisdom did not fashion Frenchmen in the image of Englishmen.' There is a wholesome general truth in this observation.

Perhaps before we turn to another subject, a word should be said about Panama. The presence of the United States on the isthmus presents a special situation which is filled with difficulties. The oligarchy which rules Panama naturally seeks to get for its people and for itself the maximum profit that flows from the presence of the canal. The administration of the canal, on the other hand, naturally balks at concession, and sometimes displays a colonialist frame of mind that is irksome to the Panamanians. In 1964 riots broke out over a trivial incident in the zone, and strident demands for the revision of the Canal Treaty of 1955 (itself a substantial concession to Panamanian sentiment) were put forth. These demands are still under negotiation as this work goes to the printer. But fundamentally, the problem is soluble. And in the background looms the question of a second canal to meet the needs of increasing traffic. This gives to the United States a considerable leverage—for not all the suggested routes for such a second canal run through Panama.

We come now to the United Nations. What is the American attitude toward this organization, and what hopes are to be entertained with regard to the organization itself? In the first place, it must be frankly admitted that the United Nations of today is not precisely the United Nations which was envisaged in 1945 at San Francisco. The collective security provisions of the charter, on which so much hope was placed at that time, seem of less and less importance. As the membership of the United Nations has been enlarged, chiefly by the admission of new states liberated from the colonial status, the tendency to neutralism has been naturally strengthened. But this is by no means to say that the charter has lost its usefulness. As we shall have occasion to say in more detail in our last chapter, there is a crying need today in the conduct of international affairs for a place where quiet discussions can take place, and friendly contacts be multiplied, without the daily intrusion of the journalist. No other institution meets this need better than the United Nations. Furthermore, there is expressed there a kind of world opinion which stresses the need for peace and accommodation.

Nor should we forget the services performed by the world organization in specific instances. The police action taken after the Suez crisis of 1956 is one example of a highly useful peace-keeping force. The operation in the Congo, though the question is more complicated, may reasonably be judged another. Though such expedients have met with opposition in the Assembly and Council, especially from the Soviet Union, though the general support of them has been denied, it is not impossible that ways will be found for more of them in the future.

Finally, the technical agencies of the United Nations do a great deal of very useful work in assembling and publishing data of much importance on world problems.

There can be no question of the interest which Americans still maintain in an organization which owes so much to the spirit of two of their great Presidents, to Woodrow Wilson and Franklin Roosevelt. What will come of their enthusiasm is, of course, impossible to predict. But it does no discredit to our people that in the harsh world of international politics they combine a severe and necessary realism with a sense of aspiration for a world more truly united in the pursuit of peace and social progress.

XIII   THE NATURE OF AMERICAN
FOREIGN POLICY TODAY

SINCE we have surveyed the foreign policy of the United States from its inception to the present day, it now behooves us to see what are its main characteristics, and what changes have taken place over nearly two centuries.

The first thing we must note is that the United States today is a military, naval, and air power of the first rank, indeed the most powerful in the world. This is a far cry from the early days of the republic, when a standing army was deemed dangerous to liberty, when a curious faith existed in the efficacy of economic pressure as a substitute for war, and when the military and naval establishments of the United States were small. The views of the fathers, moreover, remained unchanged for many, many years, as a brief survey will show. Take first the army. At the outset of the War of 1812, the total land forces of the United States amounted to about 12,000 men—this for a country of seven million. In 1846, when we went to war with Mexico, the total had actually fallen to 7640 men. The vast armies raised in the Civil War were speedily dissolved, and, by 1890, the regular army had again shrunk to a mere 27,000 men. Then came what was, from the comparative point of view, a substantial rise. By 1912 the figure for the armed forces, including the National Guard, was 213,000, one-fourth of one per cent of the total population. World War I, though it resulted in the raising of more than three and a half million troops, resulted in no substantial growth of the military establishment. By 1935, the total number of enlisted men was only 137,000, actually less than it had been twenty-three years before. In World War II the government raised something like 11,000,000 soldiers. But consistent with our long tradition, the clamor for reduction soon began. By 1948 the figure had dropped to 552,000. It was only the increasing tension with the Soviet Union which saw the development of a new military establishment, which in its ground and air forces stood in 1964 at over 1,600,000.

The story of the navy is not quite the same; in the nineteenth century, for the most part, growth was slow. But by the end of the century, substantial growth took place. Yet the United States made itself the champion, as we have seen, of naval disarmament in the 'twenties and early 'thirties, and only reluctantly increased its forces as the critical years of the 'forties drew near. The portentous power of the United States today is due to no fundamental change in the American spirit; it has been made necessary by events occurring outside our borders. Even today, the hope of disarmament remains strong in a not inconsiderable element in our population. But none of what we have just said should conceal the fact that we are now a great military power, that the role of the military inevitably has been much enhanced, that military considerations play a central role in our budget, accounting for 50 per cent of federal expenditures, and that the balance between civil and military power is not what it once was. So far we have avoided the danger of military control of policy, in the sweeping sense; and our traditions of civil authority are strong. Yet the Truman-MacArthur episode illustrates only too well how a strong-minded military man may seek to call the tune. From this point of view, the courageous act of President Truman in 1951 seems of outstanding significance.

In a second respect the nature of American foreign policy has undergone a tremendous shift since 1945. The traditional policy of the United States called, as has been made clear, for the avoidance of 'entangling alliances.' Save for the French alliance of the Revolution, this country never entered into another alliance until the period of the Second World War. Yet today it has engagements with many, many nations, with the nations of Latin America through the Rio Act of 1947, with the nations of Western Europe through NATO (1949), with the nations of Eastern Asia through the treaty of Manila (1954), with Nationalist China and with Korea. The desirability of these engagements, at least of some of them, may be questioned, but their existence is undeniable. This amounts to a revolution in the foreign policy of the United States.

In a third respect, a great change has taken place. In the nineteenth century, particularly in the last quarter of it, and whenever the Republicans were in power in the twentieth, the economic trade policy of the United States was protectionist in its bias and inspiration. But since 1933 the country has been moving, a bit irregularly, yet without serious interruption, toward the broadening of the channels of international trade. The latest illustration of this fact, already alluded to, is the Reciprocal Trade Agreements Act of 1962. The question of lower and higher tariffs is no longer a partisan one; and while reaction, of course, may come, there seems little reason at the moment to anticipate it.

Still a fourth change, which is to many persons obscure, is the integration of financial policy with that of other parts of the world, specifically with Western Europe through the Bank of International Settlement. The subject is an esoteric one, hardly suited to detailed treatment in such a treatise as this, but the fact is important. The stability of world currencies is far nearer to reality today than it was in the 'thirties or 'forties.

We may turn from considerations of this kind to questions involving the mechanism of foreign policy. It is, of course, obvious that the size of the establishment engaged in the conduct of foreign policy has been immensely enlarged; the number employed by the State Department in 1913 was only a few hundred; in 1963 over 42,000. And this does not take account of the fact that the activities of many other agencies, for example, the Federal Tariff Commission, or the preparation of the Defense budget, impinge very directly upon the work of the State Department. Nor does it take account of the newly created CIA, which, in personnel, now reaches a figure approximately that of the State Department itself. The growth of these agencies inspires a certain type of American with misgiving. There is in some quarters a feeling that the payrolls are padded, and that bureaucratic procedure stands in the way of prompt and effective action. There is also a feeling that recruitment is not satisfactory, that the government cannot command the kind of ability which is drawn into the world of business. Of course such criticisms probably conceal a modicum of truth. There *is* a question of whether too many people are employed; there is a question of slow procedure, which led such a Secretary of State as Foster Dulles to ignore his subordinates on occasion; from time to time there is error on a scale which seems to justify criticism of the ability of those concerned, as in the Bay of Pigs fiasco. But there is another side to the shield. Foreign policy is an enormously complicated business. Like virtually every important form of activity today, it requires specialized knowledge. It cannot be made 'off the cuff,' as occasionally an American politician proposes. All this means that a substantial personnel is necessary. And nothing suggests, to this writer, at any rate, that more mistakes are made in the field of diplomacy by the experts than are made by similarly placed people in other fields of activity. We need, and must have, a sophisticated view of foreign affairs, if we are to judge wisely; there is no virtue in improvisation, in hasty and emotional decisions, in action based on ignorance. One of the things that the average American citizen needs most to realize is that judgment without the data is rarely of much help in the making of policy. We shall, however, come back to the role of the citizen a little later.

Connected with the question of the growth of professionalism is the adjustment of the American constitutional mechanism to the more pressing necessities of the current world. There are two important constitutional prescriptions which may be thought to stand in the way of prompt and efficient action when such action is required. One is the rule requiring the consent of two-thirds of the Senate for the ratification of treaties. The other is the authority given to Congress, and to Congress only, to declare war.

With regard to the first of these, the actual damage done by the two-thirds rule has been, I think, less than has often been assumed; yet it is true that with different constitutional forms the hassle over admission to the League of Nations might have come out differently —and perhaps better—and there are other instances of Senatorial obstruction. But the genius of American politics has found a way around the obstacles presented by the two-thirds rule. As long ago as 1844, there being no two-thirds majority of the Senate in favor of the annexation of Texas, Texas was annexed by joint resolution. The same expedient was resorted to in the case of the annexation of Hawaii in 1898. In more recent times, Congressional legislation by ordinary majorities has been used to accomplish results which in early times might have required the use of the treaty power. Thus, for example, the lend-lease enactment of 1941 was passed as a statute. The question of foreign aid has been the subject of legislation, not of treaty agreement. Sometimes, indeed, Congress goes so far as to give to the President wide discretion in negotiating agreements with other nations. This is the case, for example, with the Reciprocal Trade Agreement Acts, which permit the Executive, with certain restrictions, to enter into tariff understanding with other powers. This authority, it should be added, has been extensively used.

There is, moreover, another weapon in the Presidential armory which diminishes the importance of the two-thirds rule. That is the power to negotiate what are called 'executive agreements.' It would be difficult to define this term. All one can say is that it is an agreement with another nation which is not submitted to the Senate. Theodore Roosevelt, as we have seen, entered into such an arrangement with the Dominican Republic in 1905. A still more striking case of the executive agreement is the famous bases-destroyer deal with Great Britain in 1940, already alluded to. The same technique was applied in April 1941 in the understandings with regard to Greenland and Iceland. Still more important, the Declaration of Washington, of January 1942, by which the war-making powers agreed not to make peace separately, was to all intents and purposes an alliance, and an alliance of great import.

Let us turn from the treaty-making power to the power to declare war. This, as we have said, is, by the Constitution, vested in Congress. But in practice the President's control over the armed forces diminishes the force of this provision. President Jefferson, for example, chastised the Barbary pirates without ever asking Congress for permission to do so. In 1844, when the treaty for the annexation of Texas was under discussion, President Tyler concentrated troops on the border and ships of war in the Gulf of Mexico, and it needed only an incident to provoke a conflict. Both President Wilson and President Roosevelt armed the merchant ships of the United States in the two wars against Germany, and President Roosevelt directed the navy to shoot German submarines on sight, all this without authority of Congress. President Truman ordered our forces into Korea without referring the question of peace or war to the national legislature. It is fair to say that the Chief Executive can, by his diplomacy, create a situation in which resort to full hostilities becomes inevitable.

An interesting phase of this matter has to do with two episodes of the Eisenhower administration. This is encouragement *in advance* to the President to use the armed forces in the assurance that his action will be sustained. In the question of Formosa, Congress authorized the Executive to use American forces in the defense of the island and its appendages. The use of the word 'authorize' troubled some of the defenders of the Executive prerogative, and when a new crisis arose with regard to Lebanon in 1957, Congress passed a resolution stating that it would *support* the President in case he found it necessary to use American force in the Middle East. A similar resolution in 1964 authorized President Johnson to act in Vietnam. What lies behind these resolutions is the growing realization of the fact that the power of decision must rest in the White House, and that in a genuine emergency Congress can hardly do otherwise than to support the leader of the nation. Putting the matter another way, though restraints exist on the Executive, ways have been found of adapting the Constitution to the necessities of the age in which we live.

Let us turn to the important and interesting question of the role of the public in foreign policy. In nothing that has been said up to this point ought it to be assumed that foreign politics is a business in which freedom of action belongs to one man, or to a few men, and in which the voice of the people is silent. This neither is nor can be true. In a democratic state, the details of policy, indeed even the major decisions, are and ought to be based on special knowledge. But these decisions have to be taken in a climate of opinion which is created by public sentiment, and which defines the limits of action. No President of the United States, for example, could launch a preventive war. The national ethos forbids it. No President could launch upon an ambitious career of foreign conquest; the deep-seated assumptions of the average American forbid it. The *tone* of our foreign policy is not set in the White House or in the State Department, but in the great body of the citizenry.

There are several ways in which this fact can be illustrated. One is the frequent insistence in American diplomacy on general principles. The average man cannot understand sophisticated differences in foreign affairs. He is therefore appealed to on general grounds. The Monroe Doctrine is one example of this fact. It is by no means easy to prove that during the nineteenth century and the early twentieth the security interests of the United States were involved in the more remote parts of Latin America; yet the famous message of Monroe was not in general conceived as having a restricted application. The Open Door Policy could be easily challenged; yet it was consistently advanced and widely accepted. The Truman Doctrine was a characteristic appeal to the general dislike of Communism. The feeling that democracy is an unqualified and generalized good plays a part in the actual evolution of policy.

Closely connected with this attachment to general principles is the ethical bias of American policy, often regarded abroad as hypocritical, but actually an expression of a deep reality. To say this, of course, is not to say that the American record is without flaw; it *does* mean that American policy is rarely cynical; that public sentiment offers a corrective to the immoderate or unscrupulous use of power; that moral conceptions enter again and again into the account, such as the reaction against imperialism, the drive for collective security, the zeal shown in many quarters for disarmament. The existence of these moral preoccupations is not always to the American interest. The moral outlook in politics can easily lead to an egregious oversimplification of the issues; and it can block the road to those concessions which are part of the difficult and dangerous business of statesmanship. A nation that never gives way on an issue because it conceives a principle to be at stake can be a very unpleasant nation to deal with, and can even defeat its own ends; a certain flexibility, a certain readiness to admit the possibility of some moral outlook other than one's own, is indispensable to the conduct of diplomacy. But along with a strong impulse to moral judgment, there is a practical and empirical side to the American mind. The moral outlook, therefore, is not necessarily a source of weakness. Indeed, it may be a source of strength in a nation ruled by the many. It may give force and drive to wise policy.

A government which must look to public sentiment for guidance will have some characteristic difficulties; it may find party division an obstacle to efficient action; it may find embarrassing the constant desire of the public to be informed—where delicate matters are under discussion. How has the United States fared in this regard?

Historically, the partisan motive has certainly played a part in American diplomacy. This was true in the discussions over the Jay Treaty; in the discussions over the acquisition of Louisiana; in the events leading up to the War of 1812; in regard to the Mexican War, and to a painful degree, in the debates over the treaty of Versailles. On the whole, however, as foreign policy has come to involve larger and larger interests, as the dangers of faction have been multiplied with the scope of American diplomacy, the record has very decidedly improved. There are some very painful episodes, of which the most striking is the one connected with the name of Senator Joseph McCarthy, who shamelessly exploited the national malaise with regard to Communism for party and personal purposes. There are still politicians who are not above denouncing every error of policy (and there will always be some errors of policy) on partisan grounds, and without the slightest constructive purpose. There will always be partisan debate in a Presidential election year. But when the chips are down, each of the postwar Presidents, from 1945 to the present day, has received bipartisan support on a substantial scale. This is true of every area, strikingly so in the case of Latin America, almost always true with regard to Europe, true with regard to the Far East. There is clamor, of course; but when the Executive appeals to Congress for support, he is likely to get it, not always in his own terms (the debates on foreign aid come to mind) but in substantial measure. And in times of real danger, the partisan element is likely to disappear.

The question of publicity is a more difficult one. Every sophisticated student of international affairs recognizes the necessity for a certain degree of secrecy; without it a crucial negotiation may be jeopardized; without it conciliation may give way to passion; without it crucial elements in the national defense may be exposed to the view of an unfriendly power. Yet it is equally necessary to recognize that in a democracy the public has a right to be informed, and that it will insist upon being informed. How shall we reconcile the conflicting considerations involved? Before answering this question, it is worth noting that no government has paid more heed to the public desire for information than that of the United States. This was true even in the early days of our diplomacy. And ever since 1861, the State Department has published volumes of diplomatic correspondence, and while these volumes are now some twenty years in arrears, they are an important indication of the general point of view. More significant is the custom, inaugurated in the days of Woodrow Wilson, of publishing contemporary correspondence. A vast amount of current negotiation is now laid before the American gaze. In addition, an active and alert press pays more attention to foreign affairs than ever before, and extracts more information from the Executive departments than would have been dreamed of twenty or thirty years ago. Finally, the debates in the United Nations play an important role in diffusing knowledge of international problems.

Has this widening of public information damaged the interests of the country? Embarrassments there sometimes have been, no doubt. But that vital positions have been surrendered because of public clamor would be very difficult to prove. And there are two considerations which ought to be borne in mind. The Soviet Union resorts not only to publicity, but to outright propaganda, and unblushing mendacity, in dealing with the questions of the moment. Is there any other answer to such machinations than open diplomacy, than the wide dissemination of information? But, in the second place, we need not assume that our government tells *everything*, or ought to tell everything. There are still channels of discourse which are secret, not only diplomatic exchanges, but the private conversations which, much to the national advantage, take place in the United Nations building in New York. There are still facts which are not revealed, and ought not to be revealed. Indeed, much goes on in the field of diplomacy which does not reach the public eye. The very vastness and complexity of the problems make this inevitable. While it is dangerous to be complacent about the matter, it seems to this author that a not unreasonable balance has been struck in our diplomacy between publicity and private discussion. We should, of course, practice restraint in public debate; our journalists should exercise restraint in the gathering and dissemination of news. But we need not feel that, up to this time, at any rate, the national interest has been seriously jeopardized by the wide scope given to the ventilation of the problems.

There are two other broad generalizations with regard to our foreign policy that need to be stated. The first has to do with the management of the American economy. While the evidence is not conclusive, it seems, as a historical matter, that our diplomacy suffers from timidity and withdrawal in a period of depression, and that it tends to be unduly aggressive in a period of recovery. It follows, therefore, that if the economy can be kept on a reasonably even keel, our foreign policy will be more consistent and better balanced. And since we have learned, and are learning, more and more about the way to achieve this result, we can be hopeful of the diplomacy of the future.

Finally, if we seek for the broad perspective that is the objective of the historian, we shall find satisfaction in the record. Naïve people, no doubt, will expect a greater degree of success than is humanly possible. Error is natural to man. In a field so complex as that of foreign affairs, it is useless to imagine that mistakes will not be made, sometimes very large mistakes. But if we compare the record of the American democracy with the record of the totalitarian states, we shall see no reason for gloom. The dictatorship of Mussolini ended in revolt and humiliation. Hitler died in the bunker in Berlin in the midst of a catastrophic defeat. The Japanese warlords grossly miscalculated, and suffered ruin. As for the Soviet Union, even within the orbit of its power, in Eastern Europe, its authority seems to be ebbing. It is losing Asia to the Chinese. It confronts a prosperous and vigorous Europe, to whose strength and prosperity the United States has made a fundamental contribution. The reaction against the Russian adventure in Cuba has been real and profound. In its economic system, Russia betrays many weaknesses as compared with the most advanced states of the West.

To say these things is no invitation to complacency. Strength, physical strength, we must have, and the courage to deploy it in case of dire necessity. Along with it we must have flexibility, seeking accommodation when we can, avoiding a dangerous rigidity. The broad view we must have, seeing our interests in the large, and in the advancement of the world economy, and not in some restricted area of our own. Peace we must strive for, as one of the great American dreams. No one can predict the future. But may we not, in contemplating the story of the past, draw hope for the years to come?

SUGGESTIONS FOR FURTHER READING

GENERAL WORKS

Bailey, Thomas A., *A Diplomatic History of the American People*, 7th ed. (New York: Appleton-Century-Crofts, 1958).
A standard text, with excellent bibliographies.

Leopold, Richard W., *The Growth of American Foreign Policy, a History* (New York: Alfred A. Knopf, 1962).
A recent text, which concentrates on the twentieth century.

Perkins, Dexter, *The American Approach to Foreign Policy*, revised ed. (Cambridge: Harvard University Press, 1962).
An analytical approach to American diplomacy, which supplements the above.

SPECIAL PERIODS

Beale, Howard K., *Theodore Roosevelt and the Rise of America to World Power* (Baltimore: Johns Hopkins Press, 1956).
Deals in depth with an interesting period. Professor Beale has a thesis which is subject to debate, but the book is well worth while, none the less.

Link, Arthur S., *Wilson the Diplomatist: A Look at His Major Foreign Policies* (Baltimore: Johns Hopkins Press, 1957).
A brief but penetrating discussion of the Wilsonian epoch.

Nevins, Allan, *The New Deal and World Affairs: A Chronicle* (New York: United States Publishers Association, 1950).
Useful for the Roosevelt years.

MacNeill, William H., *America, Britain and Russia: Their Cooperation and Conflict, 1941-1946* [Survey of International Affairs, 1939-46] (London: Oxford University Press, 1953).
Brilliant analysis of the war period.

Spanier, John W., *American Foreign Policy Since World War II*, paper ed. (New York: Frederick A. Praeger, 1960).
The best general analysis of the period.

For exploration in depth, the volumes of *The United States in World Affairs*, published annually since 1933 by the Council on Foreign Relations, are of great value.

INDEX

INDEX